BACKTRACK

Great Outdoors Books from Islandport Press

This Cider Still Tastes Funny!
by John Ford Sr.

Suddenly, the Cider Didn't Taste So Good!
By John Ford Sr.

Tales from Misery Ridge
By Paul Fournier

Where Cool Waters Flow
by Randy Spencer

My Life in the Maine Woods
by Annette Jackson

Nine Mile Bridge
by Helen Hamlin

These and other books are available at:
www.islandportpress.com

Islandport Press is a dynamic, award-winning publisher dedicated
to stories rooted in the essence and sensibilities of New England.
We strive to capture and explore the grit, heart, beauty, and
infectious spirit of the region by telling tales, real and imagined,
that can be appreciated in many forms by readers, dreamers,
and adventurers everywhere.

BACKTRACK

V. Paul Reynolds

ISLANDPORT PRESS

ISLANDPORT PRESS
P.O. Box 10
Yarmouth, Maine 04096
www.islandportpress.com
books@islandportpress.com

ISBN: 978-1-934031-64-3
Library of Congress Card Number: 2013930184

Dean L. Lunt, publisher
Book jacket design by Karen F. Hoots, Hoots Design
Book designed by Michelle Lunt, Islandport Press
Cover photo by Sandy Maceys
Author photo by Diane Reynolds

For my children, Scott, Suzanne, and Josh,
and their families, who bring me so much joy.

Table of Contents

Introduction

A *backtrack* is, quite simply, going back where you came from. I picked *Backtrack* as the title for this book because it seemed to fit my plan—to go back along the path of my life's journey and revisit some vivid outdoor experiences.

My late father, Harvard Reynolds, brought me along in the outdoors. Beginning in the late 1940s, he often took me with him when he fished and hunted his favorite haunts.

A couple of memories from those days stand out as clear as the water in a remote Maine trout pond.

I am there with him at Hatcase Pond. Hatcase was loaded with nice brookies, and, back then, it wasn't a municipal water supply. We are standing atop a huge rock with our fishing rods and worm cans. As the night crawler and gold spinner dance to the bottom of the pond, dozens of fat little trout attack our offerings. My dad, a serious man most of the time, is excited in a childlike way. His joy and enthusiasm is infectious. Working together, we stuff the creel with trout and cool them down with some wet moss from the shore. (In those days you kept trout for the pan, and the daily limit was ten, as I recall.) Memories.

1

Courtesy of V. Paul Reynolds

I was hooked on fishing at an early age. This is me at about four years old. I am ready to join Dad for "trouting" on a small trout brook not far from Bangor. The neighborhood cemetery, where we raced our Flyer snow sleds can be seen in the background if you look real close.

That same June, we fished from his Old Town square-stern boat at Spring River Lake, down near Franklin. To my delight, Dad spat on a fidgeting night crawler that he had affixed to my hook. Lowering the bait into the boat's wake, he promised that the spit would bring good luck. I caught one of the biggest brook trout I have ever caught, even to this day! Memories.

Dad and I hunted, too. Birds and deer. My father was not an exceptional deer hunter. My uncles, on my mother's side, were, however, the best when it came to putting whitetails on the game pole. I was pretty "tuned in," even at a young age, and noticed that my uncles were the real deal. Dad always went away to deer camp for a week down in Beddington with my uncles, though he rarely bagged a deer. I begged to go, to see why my dad and uncles so looked forward to that annual fall getaway.

"Someday," he said, but he never said when "someday" would come. As it turned out, I was probably still too young to go when he finally decided that "someday" had arrived.

I remember clearly. It was twilight along the Union River drainage when we opened the old battered door to deer camp and

2

stepped into a world that I had never seen before. What a hovel! The sights, the sounds, and the smells remain with me to this day. Next to the door stood a big, Clarion woodstove crackling and throwing off heat. The floor was dirt. The roof was tar paper and weathered gray boards. Steam rose from the soggy wool clothing that hung on every nail and hook above the stove. Across the room was a large gun rack that held an assortment of hunting rifles and gear. There was loud talk and glasses of amber liquid. My uncles were hunched over a big kitchen table covered with playing cards, poker chips, and ashtrays—lots of ashtrays. Smoked filled the room. Profanity like I had never heard before assaulted my ears. My uncles greeted me warmly, but somehow they seemed different. Should I really be here, I wondered?

There was also something else. Beneath the loud talk and general deer camp din, flowed an endless stream of fascinating deer-hunting stories mingled with warm fellowship. There seemed to be a manly connection. I took to it all. Memories.

From those first days in the woods and on the waters of Maine with my father, sprang my romance with the outdoors. Over the years, throughout my adult working life as disc jockey, broadcast engineer, college student, and later, as a naval officer and editor of *The Bangor Daily News*, I took to the woods and trout ponds at every opportunity. Like so many who love the outdoors, I found work too often got in the way of my hunting and fishing.

This work-versus-play conflict took a serendipitous turn when I least expected it. At the time, I was a newspaper executive who had fallen out of favor with the publisher at *The Bangor Daily News*. As a result, I involuntarily parted ways with him. Suddenly, gone was the daily newspaper that had been my workaday life and consuming passion for more than two decades. It was a difficult time for me. However, what I didn't know as those days played out was that another door was about to open, and a more exciting, fulfilling phase of my life lay just ahead.

Ray "Bucky" Owen, who was then the commissioner at the Maine Departrment of Inland Fisheries and Wildlife, chose me as his information and education officer. The job was a good fit. Bucky was a fun and dynamic man to work for. The combination of my media experience and knowledge of the outdoors came into play as I worked as a spokesman for the department. As I rubbed elbows with wardens and fish and wildlife biologists, I learned a lot about fish and wildlife policy and management, and, unknowingly, was grooming myself for a second career.

At about the time that Governor Angus King decided not to reappoint Bucky and his appointees (myself among them) to a second term, I met Vic Morin, who had founded a promising new publication called the *Northwoods Sporting Journal*. Convinced of the publication's potential and impressed with Vic's energy, I bought in as an equal partner and co-publisher. At the same time, I started writing a self-syndicated weekly outdoor column, "Outdoors in Maine," for the *Lewiston Sun Journal*, the *Northwoods Sporting Journal*, and a number of other Maine weekly newspapers. I also began cohosting a weekly outdoor radio program, *Maine Outdoors*, with well-known Millinocket guide Wiggie Robinson. Wiggie was a jewel of a man you will read about in this book.

Wiggie was a friend and mentor, not unlike my father. My dad, a Bangor and Houlton businessman who managed oil businesses for Dead River Company, was proud of his upward mobility. As a young family, early on, we didn't have much materially, not by today's standards. Growing up in a poor neighborhood, oddly enough, left me with wonderful, vivid memories. We made our own fun. There were no electronic diversions. Winter or summer, outside play was the norm from dawn to dusk. There might have been some lunch breaks for a peanut butter

Courtesy of V. Paul Reynolds

In later years, I have returned a number of times to southern Aroostook county to fish the kettle ponds, where dad and I fished back in the 1950s. This is me with an ice-out brookie taken while trolling a Mickey Finn. Friend and fishing partner, Gifford Stevens, is the stern man.

and jelly sandwich, but the rest of time we were thoroughly engaged out of doors. There was no such thing as boredom. We played baseball or war with homemade wooden guns. In winter, we skated and raced our sleds among the headstones in the cemetery near Ohio Street. There were colorful butterflies to catch in nets made from onion bags. The butterflies were mounted on old boards, alongside the skins of innocent little chipmunks that I had dispatched with my Daisy BB gun. In my early teens, with my father's help and guidance, I built and raced a soap box derby that set a statewide speed record and first place win at the 1953 annual Brewer Soap Box Derby race. My derby, "The Ole Lucky 7," made a respectful showing at the national soap derby box races in Akron, Ohio. That same year we moved to Houlton. My sisters missed Bangor. But for me the Shiretown was a good fit. Dad and I fished and hunted the streams and kettle ponds in southern Aroostook County. Picking potatoes for $.25 a barrel on frosty October mornings, and getting out of school to do it, was the cat's meow! To this day, I still can smell the damp earth and hear the clackety-clack of the digger behind the big tractor.

My mother, Helen, who apparently saw something in my youthful obsession to learn new things, taught me to focus my artistic side. At her urging I immersed myself in oil painting and amateur radio. At 15, I became a fully licensed ham radio operator and from my attic on School Street in Houlton I sometimes talked to other ham operators as far away as Australia. When I was a high school sophomore, our family move back to Bangor. After graduating from Bangor High School in 1958, I attended Grantham School of Electronics in Washington, D.C and soon after worked in the Bangor media market as a disc jockey and television news anchor. Six years later, after a checkered academic experience, I managed to graduate from the University of Maine.

Photo by Jud Powell

At the University of Maine I chased deer more than I did co-eds, at least in November. This photo was taken at Tomah Flowage, not far from Vanceboro. A college buddy, Jud Powell, and I hunted this sprawling flowage from his dad's deer camp.

Between college and Naval Officer Candidate School in Newport Rhode Island, I worked behind the bar at the infamous Green Door in Bar Harbor. Soon my college sweetheart, Diane Davis, and I became engaged. We were later married in Barrington, Rhode Island. We started our family in Virginia Beach, Virginia during the Vietnam War where I served three years of active duty at the Oceana Naval Air Station.

In 1967, Diane and I made an important decision. The U.S. Navy wanted to send me to graduate school, all expenses paid in exchange for a five-year re-enlistment. But Maine beckoned. We wanted our children to grow up in Maine, as we did. By

Christmas of that year, we were homeward bound, permanently. It was a good move.

Much of this book is about friends and family—hunting partners and fishing buddies without whom there really would not have been so many indelible memories. Some of my most valued outdoor experiences have been fishing, hunting, and camping with my three children and my wife, Diane, who is a capable outdoorswoman in her own right. Together, she and I have hiked, hunted, and fished not only most of Maine, but much of North America as well. One of my close friends to this day was once the cook at my University of Maine fraternity house, Beta Theta Pi, in 1963. The cook and I have hunted and fished—and shared our lives—for more than fifty years. You'll meet him, in chapter 49. He is one of a number of close outdoor companions who belong to a long-enduring deer-hunting organization we call the Skulkers of Seboeis, which also gets a cameo mention in this book. Over more than forty years at deer camp, the Skulkers, characters all, furnished me with enough column fodder to last almost another lifetime. I wrote about them in my first book, *Maine Deer Hunter's Logbook*.

Along with forging lasting friendships, time spent fishing and hunting is also about seeing new country and honing new skills. In the outdoor-writing business, editors often pay particular homage to what we refer to as "how-to stories." You know—how to get a fire started in the rain, how to use a compass, or skin a deer. You'll find quite a lot of how-to stuff in this book. I hope it will be useful. Most of the best ideas or outdoor skills are ones that I learned from others. In some cases, credit is given. In others, the mentors, for practical reasons of space, will go unnamed. To all of the wonderful friends and outdoor companions with whom I have shared a warming fire or a duck blind, thank you, one and all.

Before you join me, and my outdoor companions, on my backtrack, please shake hands with Fred Benton, a California outdoor writer. Fred agreed to let me use his carefully chosen, thoughtful words that I think will serve well as an invocational prelude to a book of this kind. Fred writes:

> Pondering the blessings of a lifelong love affair with the outdoors is humbling. It brings a little moisture to the eyes. It brings this simple thought: Thank you, Lord, for all that you have given me as a hunter. For the mountains, real and imaginary. For the joyful days of good health and freedom in wild places. For great friends and hunting partners. For the magnificent creatures it has been my privilege to hunt. Not all hunts were successful, but every day spent hunting was good as gold.
>
> If my luck holds, someday when the old legs and ticker falter, as they must, I can rear back in my rocker and, whenever I choose to, climb up there again—way up at timberline in the Bittersweets, close to the sun, with the wind in my face, a rifle in my hand, and a laugh for all the world's troubles.

Happy trails!

Part I:

Adventures

1

The Old Aeronca

My wife says that caring too much for inanimate things is
not the grown-up thing to do. She has a point. I mean, face it: a
Polaris 550, a Dodge Ram, or even a Jiffy ice auger is not going
to love you back no matter how nice you are to it.

She resented my old airplane, because my flying worried her.

It was a faded yellow tail-dragger, a cloth-covered Aeronca
L-3. First used to train army pilots in the 1940s, it was a simple
machine—stick and rudder. There was no radio. Instruments
included a tachometer, airspeed indicator, altimeter, compass, oil
pressure gauge, and a turn-and-bank indicator. The gas gauge
was a small glass tube mounted near the trim handle. Powered
by a 60-horsepower motor that sounded like an old farm tractor,
you started it by flipping the wooden propeller after a few slow
turns for prime. Prone to ground loop, keeping it straight on
takeoffs and landings was the toughest part of flying it. Once in

the air, it was easy to fly, as plodding and predictable as an old draft horse.

I remember the old Aeronca always in the springtime. Flying it before work, early in the mornings of April and May, was a joyful thing. Climbing off the ground on a still, windless morning, just as the sun peeked over the hills of Dedham, in a noisy, near-antique airplane imparted a sense of freedom that was hard to get across to my wife. Picture it. The Eastern horizon is a red glow, and beneath you the newly budded hardwoods spatter the ground with a lime-green lushness. The rumbling, throaty engine is throttled back to 2,000 rpms. You slide back the Plexiglas side window and the cool morning air from the slipstream clears your head of earthly matters.

I was fond of that airplane. But ownership of it was not without complications.

Once on a return flight from ice-fishing at Chemo Pond, my nephew and I ran into freezing rain. With the ice-laden windscreen obscuring my forward vision, we managed to get the airplane back to Brewer and on the ground by looking out the side windows. My nephew's voice changed an octave during that flight, and he never flew with me again.

That same winter, during a bumpy solo hop to Seboeis Lake, a snow squall began pounding me over Alton. While struggling to maintain airspeed and get the airplane's skis onto Boyd Lake, my backseat passenger—a pair of pickerel snowshoes—fell off the backseat and got jammed between the seat and the rear control stick. The situation became awkward. Since the front and rear control sticks are wired together, I suddenly lost pitch-up control of the flailing yellow bird. (This is not good, and especially not good under windy, limited-visibility conditions.) Thankfully, my luck held. After some hair-raising moments, I

Photo by Jack Loftus

The Aeronca L-3 after "catching an edge" during a soft-field landing at the Brewer airstrip. The author walked away unscathed, except for his wounded pride.

was able to reach back, hold up the snowshoes with my right hand, and control a landing with my left hand.

Eventually, my relationship with this old machine ended with a crash.

In early April, during a soft-field practice landing in Brewer, the right tire on the main landing gear bogged down in some mud during the landing rollout. The Aeronca and I did a gentle somersault in full view of three golfers. As I hung upside down contemplating my next move, the white-faced, bug-eyed golfers peeked in and queried, "Are you awright?"

I was fine, but the Aeronca sustained cuts and bruises and a badly bent wing strut and propeller.

15

The jig was up.

There was no way to hide this one from my wife, or downplay the bad landing. The newspaper where I worked ran a large photo of the airplane on its back in the mud, looking very undignified.

My short-lived career as a bush pilot came to an abrupt end a short time later during one of those serious kitchen-table discussions that husbands and wives sometimes have.

The Aeronca L-3? It's doing just fine. I patched it up with a new prop and a welded wing strut I dredged up from Lucky LaChance over in St. Albans. A guy named Jim bought the airplane from me for about what I paid for it. Jim and his wife flew it until a bad windstorm broke the tie-downs and dinged it up again. Jim then sold the craft to a guy in Bowdoinham. Word is that the sixty-year-old flying machine is still airworthy.

What I wouldn't give to see her—I mean "it"—again. I would do a slow walk around and run up the engine for old times' sake. And perhaps, if the weather was right, the airplane's new owner would let me take a few turns around the pattern.

2

Trouble on the Mountain

Adam Moore guided his quarter horse down the narrow, rocky trail. It was almost lunchtime. A soft October breeze stirred the golden aspen leaves. Beyond the dark scrub oak, the valley spread out like a green carpet. Above the valley, the black-green timber spiraled up and up into the razor-blue Colorado sky. Moore, saddle-weary and dust-caked, sucked in a lungful of clear mountain air. He reminded himself to stop daydreaming, to concentrate on the business at hand. The wiry, young elk-hunt outfitter turned in his saddle. Looking back, he tugged at the rope on his lead mule and urged the pack mules down the mountainside.

Moore's reverie was broken by an unexpected sight that unnerved him. Coming up the trail from the basin below was another wrangler he knew all too well—an illegal outfitter from Missouri. The man from Missouri had had words with Adam and his dad during last fall's elk season. He was not an easy person to forget. The Missourian was conducting an unlicensed and illegal guiding operation, and doing it in an area where the Moores had paid the government year after year for the right to operate a business exclusively in that area. Adam knew that the Missouri interloper was trouble. Word was out among the other legitimate outfitters that this was a tough hombre, and that, as a convicted felon, it was illegal for him to even possess firearms, let alone to guide elk hunters.

Moore's stomach churned. As the man rode closer with his "sports" trailing behind, anger took over.

"Those better be your relatives you're guiding, man," Adam blurted out, perhaps not thinking. Maybe sensing the sudden tension in the air, Adam's mules balked. As he turned back to check the mules, the Missourian's right fist came out of nowhere and pummeled Adam twice in the face.

"You sonuvabitch," the illegal outfitter hissed. "I'll kill you and your old man if it's the last thing I ever do," the man screamed, with his hand clasping the grip of his holstered sidearm.

Stunned and bleeding, but still in the saddle, Adam left the scene as fast as he could manage with his pack mules in tow.

Back at base camp, we helped Adam off his horse and tied up his mules. The elk guide was badly beaten and sick to his stomach. As Diane and I worked to ease his discomfort, Adam's guides and wranglers were talking seriously about vigilante justice, but a cooler head prevailed. Adam's father, Paul, a partner in the elk-outfitting operation, calmed the wranglers down. Before heading to Craig General Hospital with Adam, Paul contacted the Moffat County sheriff's office.

Before Paul left, he sent me back up the mountain on horseback with my apron and Teflon cookware. The family emergency had called Paul away from his party of six elk hunters, who were awaiting their evening meal at a spike camp up in elk

country. My nag Spot and I, relieved not to have met the man
from Missouri on our way up the rocky trail, found the spike
camp in time to, as they say in those parts, "rustle up some
grub" for six hungry Pennsylvanians.

*Colorado elk guide and wrangler Greg Spickler shares an intimate
moment with my mount Spot not long after law officers took away a
Missouri troublemaker in handcuffs. Spickler guided the lawmen to the
bad guy's elk camp.*

During the night, howling coyotes apparently spooked old Spot, who was tied to an aspen tree. A known knot picker, Spot was nowhere to be seen come daybreak.

Minus Spot, I hoofed it alone back to base camp in time to see a Colorado game warden and three Moffatt County deputy sheriffs donning flak jackets and preparing to ride back up the hill that I had just come down. They were armed to the teeth with Big Irons on their hips, AR-15s slung on their backs, and ammo clips strapped to their legs. One of our camp wranglers— unarmed—was delegated to lead the law to the camp of the man from Missouri.

The story has a pretty good ending. After a morning stakeout of his spike camp, the man from Missouri gave up without a fight. He was apprehended while watering his stock. Not a single shot was fired. The law brought him down off the mountain on horseback with his hands cuffed behind him. Adam recovered from his wounds, although not without some bone damage and discomfort.

Charged with multiple counts, including aggravated assault and criminal threatening with a firearm, the Missourian was tried and wound up where he belonged—behind bars. There are no doubt lessons for all of us in this story, but the lesson for the enforcement division of the Colorado Wildlife Department is to pay closer attention when hardworking, law-abiding outfitters like the Moores complain about illegal activities. For two years, the Missouri felon guided elk hunters illegally in Colorado with impunity. Before resorting to violence, this felon flouted the law and undermined the livelihood of honest outfitters. Somebody could have been killed.

Spot? He eventually found his way back to base camp, although I worried a lot about that horse, especially after a cowboy practical joker named Kendall had me convinced that Spot had most likely been shot by a novice elk hunter.

Photo by Diane Reynolds

My lost horse, Spot, was eventually found and returned to our elk camp. The boss forgave me for losing my mount. Another horse—one that was not a knot picker—was made available to me for the hunt, after the camp chores were done.

21

3

Lost on Schoodic Lake

Outdoor friends are special. It doesn't really matter where in the outdoors you spend time together. Whether sharing the bone-chilling cold in a coastal duck blind during the second season, struggling to get a 180-pound deer out of a fir swamp, or simply sharing stories by a well-kindled campfire, you share an unspoken bond.

Among those I have enjoyed the outdoors with over the years, there is one who has, shall we say, a penchant for adventure. No, that's being charitable. This guy over the years has gotten us into trouble. Not with the law. Not with our wives. Not that kind of trouble. I mean, outdoor trouble. You know the kind: His outboard motor quits eight miles from camp when you are beating your way back in a summer squall. He gets the four-wheel-drive truck mired trying to get you both into a trout pond on a road that would challenge a good skidder.

In early April, he talks you into staying one more night at his remote camp for some next-day ice-fishing and a warm rain overnight washes out the snowmobile trail.

Let's call my outdoor friend "Ron." Ron means well. A capable outdoorsman in most respects, but cursed with a "trouble gene" at birth—outdoor trouble seems to follow Ron around like a faithful old bird dog. In fact, since our first calamitous ice-fishing trip at Northwest Pond in 1967, we have gotten into so many fixes that at the conclusion of our outings one of us will invariably smile at the other and say, "Well, we cheated death again."

Obviously, the "cheating death" comment is intended as a witticism, an acknowledgment of the unspoken bond and our swashbuckling Walter Mitty streaks. There was one trip, though, when neither of us joked about cheating death.

The forecast called for snow. Flurries were predicted for Friday night into Saturday morning, with some lingering snowfall in higher elevations. The outlook for Sunday and Washington's Birthday was clear and cold. Not ones to shy away from a little snowfall or cold weather, we decided the trip was a go.

Our destination that weekend was Ron's small cabin at the south end of Seboeis Lake. Getting there with wives, kids, and three days' worth of dunnage was never easy. Back in those days of the 12-horsepower, single-cylinder Skidoos, the best access to Seboeis Lake in the winter was via Schoodic Lake. Seboeis Lake is just a few miles east of Schoodic Lake. By parking our trucks and trailers at the landing at Lakeview, we could then take our snowmobile convoy up the east shore of Schoodic until we came to the Carry Trail, which cuts across through the woods to the southwest shore of Seboeis Lake. From there, it was a quick run across the lake to Ron's lakeside cabin.

So there we were, that February weekend. Two families intent on another wintertime weekend together at camp. That

Saturday morning we arrived at Lakeview, and after being assured by some local folks that there was plenty of blue ice, we decided to drive our cars and snowmobile trailers part way up the east shore before unloading our machines and gear for the trip in.

Soon, after wives Val and Diane got the four kids outfitted and Ron and I got the tote sleds loaded with sleeping bags, extra gas, and food, the convoy departed for camp. Mr. Bombardier would have been proud. Two 12-horsepower Skidoos hauled nicely two teams each comprising a husband and wife, two pint-sized kiddos, and a tote sled heavy with gear.

By the time we covered the eight or nine miles to Ron's camp, the weather was taking on a slightly new look. Mid-afternoon found us all warm and fed as a fire crackled in the big ramdown stove. Our four- and five-year-olds munched candy bars and played games atop the big double bunks in Ron's one-room camp. Outside, though, the weather was worsening. A stiffening wind had swung around to the northeast, and the weatherman's forecast of occasional snow flurries had become a total whiteout.

Concerned that our vehicles and trailers would become snowbound where they were parked two or three miles up the big lake, Ron and I decided to snowmobile to the cars, drive them back to the Lakeview parking lot, and then snowmobile back to camp by suppertime. Diane and Val agreed to keep the home fires burning. We struck out.

As we came out of the Carry Trail and started out onto the big lake, the winter storm announced its presence. Atop the ice, there was a good six to eight inches of snow where that morning there might have been a few inches. The wind howled down the lake. When we arrived at the cars, the drifts were already piling up around the trailers.

We loaded our Skidoos and began the drive down the lake. The going was slippery and slow. Soon both cars were stuck on the lake about a half-mile from the Lakeview parking lot. As it began to get dark, we decided to abandon the cars and make for camp. Our wives would be worried. We headed north up the lake.

Darkness overtook us, and soon, so did the storm. It was a classic winter nor'easter. A 30-knot wind and a dropping thermometer pushed the unrelenting fine snow sideways. In a rush to get back to camp, we struck a straight course up the lake. Our Skidoos chugged along nicely, but soon the tree line on the east shore was not visible in the wind-driven snow. My eyeglasses became encrusted with water and ice. The headlight on my '64 Skidoo began to blink on and off. I fell in behind Ron's snowmobile and hugged his red taillight. Close to an hour passed. I began to worry . . . really worry.

Low on gas and plagued by zero visibility and only one headlight between us, our zest for adventure was dampened by the sobering realization that we were going in circles somewhere on a lake twelve miles long. Like a boater lost in a fog bank without a compass, we were going nowhere.

"I can't find the damn tree line," Ron shouted over the storm and the rattle of his snow-sled engine. As we stopped to take stock of our situation, I told Ron that I was having all I could do to stay with his weak taillight, let alone see the tree line.

"I think we should head that way," Ron yelled, pointing at right angles to the driving snow. "Whaddya think?"

Nodding in agreement, it wasn't until much later that I told him what I'd really thought: *We are flat-out lost. This is one mean storm. By now, Diane is worried sick. Hell, we could freeze to death right here tonight in the middle of Schoodic Lake. Why do I get in these situations with you? We need a break.*

The break did come, and none too soon. Nearly four hours after we'd begun what we expected to be a thirty-minute trip back to our families awaiting us at Seboeis Lake, we spotted the

Ron Hastie (left) and Maine Guide Doug Russell check duck nesting boxes at Seboeis Lake, not far from where Hastie and the author got lost at night in a blizzard on Schoodic Lake.

tree line along Schoodic's east shore and soon found the opening to the Carry Trail that leads to Seboeis Lake.

Cold, wet, tired, and almost out of gas, we sighed and smiled with relief when we saw the gaslights shining through the camp windows.

When we stumbled half frozen into the camp, our wives, ready with hugs, were relieved on a number of counts. They didn't seem to mind that we did begin to drip and melt before the kitchen stove like two thawing refugees from the Ice Age.

They wonderered for hours "Where are they?" as they watched darkness descend and the late February storm blow up across the lake. With our young children huddled under sleeping bags in the bunks of an uninsulated camp and the mercury dropping on the porch thermometer, they had fretted that the modest wood stove and cherry red stove pipe were working harder then they should have been. They were right. Soon, though, with the stove and our adrenaline under control, we recounted to all our winter adventure in the Schoodic Lake whiteout.

The kids loved being marooned in the storm, and still talk about to this day.

After a couple of days, it cleared, and our old Skidoos took all of us uneventfully back down the lake on one of those sparkling clear mornings when it's great to be alive. Someone with a front-end loader opened a path to our buried cars. We were told that another snowmobiler had perished on the lake.

Today, more than forty years later, Ron and I still conspire together on outdoor adventures. We still get into some tricky situations, and one of us will invariably make the observation on the way home: "Hey, we cheated death again."

But we nearly didn't that night when we were lost on Schoodic Lake.

4

The Lightning Thing

Throughout the ages, man has long been both fascinated and frightened by lightning—nature's discharge of electricity. The Greeks saw Zeus as the god of weather, a bewhiskered, powerful icon who clutched a thunderbolt and ruled from Mount Olympus. According to scientists, who are still debating its exact genesis, a bolt of lightning travels at an incredible velocity, 60,000 miles per second. And talk about hot; when lightning strikes the Earth, its temperature is 54,000 degrees Fahrenheit! Each year there are 16 million lightning strikes around the world. Weather people record locations of lightning strikes in the United States annually.

Although Maine is not, according to weather statistics, a lightning-intense state, anyone who spends enough time in the outdoors will sooner or later have a close encounter with lightning. It can be downright scary.

A few years ago, in early September, I tried to outrun an incoming electrical storm coming hell-bent down a lake. The wall of the storm cell was about five miles north of my boat and sweeping my way. Camp and shelter from the impending deluge was a mere mile away. If my 6-horsepower Johnson outboard had been a 20-horsepower, I might have made it.

But I didn't. The September squall descended in all its fury. Amid the lightning, driving rain, and crashing thunder, the stench of ozone announced the proximity of the electrical activity. As I willed my outboard to go faster and my heart to beat slower, the squall cell passed, leaving me cowed but unscathed.

Yes, I was foolish, and lucky. I broke a cardinal rule: In an electrical storm, don't get caught on the water. It just wasn't my time.

Although there is a level of vulnerability for any person caught in the outdoors in an electrical storm, there are measures that you can take to reduce the risk of being struck. *Northwoods Sporting Journal* survival writer Charlie Reitze has given this issue a lot of careful thought. Here are some of Charlie's lightning-avoidance tips, extracted from a recent column:

> Stay away from open areas. If you're in an open area where you're the tallest object, then the lightning is coming after you, as it is attracted to the tallest objects. Find a low-altitude, closed-in area with low-growth timber. Shed your backpack. Get away from it. If you're with someone else, get away from them. The object is to make the smallest possible target. Two people together make a bigger target than one. Don't lie down thinking that your being closer to the ground will make you a lesser target. Wrong! Bad wrong! When you lie down, you give the lightning a much bigger area to strike. The closeness to the ground isn't what's going to make the difference

where people are concerned; the smallest you can make yourself is. So after getting as far away from your pack as is reasonable and shedding your metal belt buckle, scooch down on your feet, keep your feet together, and bend your

Photo by V. Paul Reynolds

When the dark storm clouds move in on any body of water, it's time to get to shore, fish or no fish!

head down. You're kind of in a squatting fetal position. This position makes you as small a target as you can get.

Unless you're a big person this position only gives the lightning a 2-foot-wide area to strike. If you're terribly concerned about keeping dry, put on a poncho or some other waterproof gear. You can even put a tarp over you and tuck in all the edges so it's as small as you can make it and stay under it. The object is to have the smallest exposed area that you can.

Lastly, if you have any inkling that there is a thunderstorm even beyond the foreseeable distance, you need to begin taking precautions. Lightning strikes often travel horizontally for long distances even before you see any rain or threatening clouds. For my money, when you hear thunder off in the distance, start making plans. Locate a safe place, put your packs someplace a good distance from where you are, get yourself set so you'll be as comfortable as possible, then when the storm comes, get in your scooching position and wait it out.

5

Calamities of the Call

Patrick McManus, one of America's foremost outdoor humorists who gets paid well to write his funny stuff, was asked to give advice to budding outdoor writers. Among his tips: "Writing about funny things that happen to you in the outdoors is a hard way to get laughs. Much better to recount your outdoor disasters." He says that people, for some reason, seem to enjoy the bad breaks of their fellows—especially when things go awry in the outdoors.

I don't know if Mr. McManus is right or not. If you're like me, you've had a lot of things go wrong while attempting to relax in the Great Outdoors. And they sure didn't seem funny at the time.

My experience with using wild-animal calls as a tool of the hunt has not always been good. In fact, with the exception of a duck call, I hunted for years without ever employing a call. Then, a few years ago, while tracking a deer on a foggy morning after a fresh snowfall, I ran out of steam and decided to rest a spell. Sitting on a stump overlooking a fir thicket, I sipped hot coffee from a thermos. A never-used deer grunt that had been given to me as a Christmas gift was hanging around my neck. Just for the heck of it, I decided to shatter the snow-laden still-ness with a couple of buck grunts.

Graaaahhh . . . graaaahhh . . .

To my shock, the grunts drew an instant response. The fir thicket below me exploded as though an elephant had been pro-voked. A large bull moose came charging up the hill toward me. Jumping up, I shouted warnings at the incoming moose. As the spilled coffee seared my gloveless hand and my knees got rub-bery, this big brown freight train stayed on track. I yelled louder and cussed at the cranky old critter.

He put on the brakes about twenty yards from my trembling form. Pawing the ground, he rocked his head with his shovel-like antlers swaying in the morning mist. I talked softly to the moose and told him not to come any closer. In my best John Wayne tone, I said that I carried a big stick, and showed the irritated creature my .35 caliber Marlin with the hammer at the ready.

Strong words worked. Not a shot was fired. Soon he turned and walked slowly away, stopping once to turn his powerful neck and cast me a parting gaze. That affair sort of turned me off to deer calls.

This one fall, though, a high-quality moose call seemed an indispensable accoutrement if I was to guide my son and wife on their first moose hunt. I bought a Buck Expert moose call. It worked well—until the last day of the hunt. On that day, it worked too well.

My son Josh, who had been abandoned by his subpermittee midweek, had hunted hard for his moose. Insisting on a trophy, he had turned down a number of moose early in the week only

Photo by Diane Reynolds

The author talking moose talk at Ross Stream.

to get anxious as he found himself mooseless on the last day. He turned to Dad.

"Let's hit the big bog," I suggested. "It'll be a haul if you get a moose down in there, Josh, but we can always quarter it up."

It was a hike to the bog, but I had always seen moose there during deer season. As the bog came in sight, I handed Josh the

Buck Expert moose call and repaired to the nearest smooth-barked tree for morning relief. While awaiting my call of nature, Josh strolled the remaining twenty yards or so to the bog's edge.

To my surprise, son Josh—who is an intuitive, calculating young man most of the time—interrupted my reverie with a single call from the moose horn. To my even greater surprise, an answer came back. The mixed hardwoods to my left exploded with mass and motion. No question. A moose incoming! It was déjà vu all over again. There was I, squatted treeside and caught pantless as the largest moose either of us had ever seen came running full bore right at me. The bull—perhaps sensing my helpless vulnerability—stopped his territorial lunge a mere thirty yards from my squatting position.

I remained motionless, frozen in a state of disbelief. The moose glared.

"Why aren't you shooting, Josh?" I whispered to myself. "You must have heard this freight train crashing through the brush." Turning my head slowly to the right in Josh's direction, I caught my son's quizzical glance. At first, Josh saw only my wide-eyed expression, my pursed lips shaping the letters M-O-O-S-E, and, of course, my pale behind lurking just below the Maine Guide patch on my green wool jacket.

Then, in the same instant, he and the moose made eye contact. There was no time for the shot. Josh's trophy moose bolted away with a speed and agility I thought reserved only for whitetails. We tracked the high-tailing moose for a half-hour or so, but never saw him again.

We covered every inch of that bog for the rest of the day, and used that potent moose call with great discretion. But when the sunset signaled the end to Josh's weeklong hunt, we both knew in our hearts that the moose hunt really had ended earlier that morning when we were both caught by surprise.

6

Maine Moose Attacks

Can you imagine what it's like to be on the receiving end of a moose charge? As I've mentioned, it happened to me while deer hunting. The bull that challenged me was provoked, apparently, by my deer-grunting calls. Obviously, I lived to tell about it. My bull was being territorial during the post-rut season.

A few winters ago there were at least two cases of snowmobilers being charged by moose. The unusually deep snow had driven moose onto the packed-down snow-sled trails. The big critters refused to be driven off the snowmobile trails and were willing to fight to stay on the "high ground."

In one incident, a man and wife on a snow sled in northern Maine were attacked when they tried to pass a moose on a trail. The wife was knocked off the sled by the moose's head. She was frightened, but not seriously hurt.

Illustration by Mark McCollough

As any wildlife biologist will tell you, a bull moose in rut can be aggressive and unpredictable. In all my years hunting, fishing and camping in the Maine woods, I have only been the focus of one moose "charge." They always look large and imposing, even when they are minding their own business. Take it from me, one annoyed bull coming straight at you is a memorable experience, but not worth repeating!

The other incident involved my oldest son, Scott Reynolds, and his ice-fishing buddy, Greg Goodman, both of Winterport. Both men were on a snow-sled trail after dark, heading into my camp at a lake in Piscataquis County. Here is my son's account, in his own words:

By 10:30 p.m. we made the trailhead and looked forward to ten miles of perfect snowmobiling to get us to our cozy camp. Thirty degrees, no wind, and two inches of fresh snow would make for a fabulous ride. Four miles into the woods, we came upon a steaming pile of moose droppings and a glistening wet bed. The big bed spanned the trail, with one set of tracks heading toward our destination. The snow in the woods was hip-deep just one step off the trail.

About a thousand yards later, the glow of my Skidoo's headlamp illuminated the black rump of a healthy moose, loping easily at twenty-five yards. I have great respect for these animals, as they endure a long, hard winter. I decided to stop, rather than stress the animal. We stopped and enjoyed the quiet night for a bit, hoping the moose would find another trail.

Another half a mile and we were back in contact with the animal. Another wait, then we continued at a snail's pace. Approaching what we affectionately call "Stink Bog," we caught up with the moose for the third and final time. Bullwinkle decided that he was far enough from his bedroom. It was time to challenge his pursuers. His body language spoke loud and clear.

A bull sheds his antlers in early winter and is not nearly as intimidating as the same animal in September, with his majestic head gear. However, standing only feet from my idling machine, illuminated by the headlight, his ears were pressed flat back along a lowered head, his eyes like slits and neck hair straight up . . . He was plenty scary.

My heart was pounding like a jackhammer and we were out of options, with no way to turn around in the narrow trail. He approached three times as he pondered his alternate path—deep snow. Finally, with his massive head hanging over the front of my sled and hot breath pouring out of each flared nostril, I bailed off the snow-mobile into the snow and frantically unsheathed my pathetic defense: a Snow & Nealley ax.

From my shaking knees behind the machine, I watched in awe as this beautiful and normally shy animal reared up on his hind legs, like a rodeo bull, and stomped to death my trusty old Skidoo. His front hooves shattered the windshield and dislocated the handlebars. The rear hooves snapped the bumper like a matchstick as he bounded up and over the sled within two feet of my head.

Reflexively, I raised the ax high as he roared past, then watched helplessly as the moose trampled Greg's sled, killing the engine and headlight. In the glare of Greg's light, I couldn't tell if he was safely out of the way. When the engine died, it was pitch black back there, and I thought Greg might be hurt, or worse.

I yelled Greg's name into the dark, praying the moose had had enough. Greg emerged from the dark holding the remains of his battered windshield.

"Are you okay?" I asked.

He replied with a calm "Yup."

I said, "Drop that thing and let's get the #$@%*& outta here!"

My heart had slowed a bit after two miles at speed, so I shut down to discuss the whole episode with Greg and take stock of the damage. Under the now-quiet blanket of a moonless night, we recounted what we had just witnessed, and thanked God for surviving unscathed. Our voices and hands were shaking and the laughter nervous.

Thinking there was no way we could repeat this experience, we continued the last two miles with a keen eye for signs. Wouldn't you know, a mile farther we encountered another nearly identical bull. The pause-and-follow routine ended abruptly when this one turned with purpose at about fifty yards and showed little caution as he approached.

Quick students, we pulled as far off the trail as possible and buried ourselves in the thick firs. Bullwinkle's cousin trotted past within two feet of the running sleds and disappeared into the darkness.

Adrenaline is fun to a point, but we'd had enough and just wanted a warm fire and a cold drink. The last mile seemed to take forever, and every corner was unnerving, but we made it. Hunting camp and the warmth of its blazing hardwood fires have never been sweeter than that midnight of Easter 2008.

7

Planning an Elk Hunt

If breathtaking scenery and big-game hunting stir your passion, consider a Colorado elk hunt. I've done it three times now: once on my own, once as a paying customer of an outfitter, and once as a working vacationer for that same elk outfitter. Each trip I brought home a pocketful of memories and some new friendships. Two out of three times I also brought back some generous elk loins for the freezer.

Perhaps you are at the stage I was a few years ago. You've toyed with the idea in the back of your mind, but haven't quite dared to take the plunge. Maybe a Colorado elk hunt has been kicked around among your fellow hunters at a Maine deer camp. "We'll do it one day," you say to each other. But the years tick off and the aspiration just lies dormant there on the dream shelf, waiting for one of you to move on it.

Having enjoyed my elk hunts so much, I can't resist encouraging you to swing into action—to seize the moment, as they say. Maybe this will help you to take the dream off the shelf and make it a reality.

Other Western states offer elk hunts, but Colorado is your best choice, and best chance of drawing an elk permit. Colorado has four rifle seasons. Your best bet is to be there for opening day of the first season. There are two ways to get an elk permit. One is by entering the spring draw through application. The other is to take your chances and purchase an over-the-counter permit when you get there. I recommend that you participate in the draw. The odds of drawing either a cow tag or a bull tag are exceptionally good. So far I've never been denied an elk permit in the spring draw.

A nonresident cow tag is about $350 and a nonresident bull tag is $500. The tag is your license. There are no other licenses or permits required. The application requires you to demonstrate that you have passed a Maine hunter-safety course, unless you were born before 1949. If you want to participate in an elk draw, you must submit your application by the deadline. You can call the Colorado Department of Wildlife (DOW) for information or to request a booklet at (303) 297-1192, or you can apply for an elk permit online at wildlife.state.co.us.

The toughest decision you will have to make is whether to freelance (go on your own) or hire an outfitter. As mentioned above, I have done it both ways. Let's review both options.

Obviously, freelancing is the least expensive. You can drive, as we did, to western Colorado with your tent and gear for about $800 round-trip (for gas and tolls). We put in long highway days and bunked at a couple of KOA campgrounds en route. Where to camp and hunt when you get there? Elk are everywhere in Colorado, but I'd suggest that you pick one of the many national forests that are west of Denver. (You will need to select a hunt area, called a Wildlife Management Unit, WMU, when you submit your application for the elk draw.) The DOW website will explain all of this.

Total costs? During my first freelance Colorado adventure, five of us did the whole trip for about $1,000 each.

The other option is to hire an outfitter. Cost-wise, this can run the gamut from as low as $1,600 to as much as $10,000. What I will outline for you here is what I know to be the best and least-expensive outfitter option.

On our second Colorado trip, we contracted with an outfitter out of Craig, Colorado, for what is called a *drop-camp hunt*.

Here's how it works: We arrived at the trailhead near a national forest and the outfitter took us and our gear by mule and horseback about twelve miles up into the high country, where a spike tent is provided. This is strictly a no-frills deal. The outfitter provides water, the tent, cooking gear, and some hunting advice. They also check up on you and take you and your elk back to the trailhead. But—and this is the best part—they place you smack dab in the middle of elk. Lots of elk.

The outfitter that we used gets $1,600 per hunter for the drop-camp hunt. This includes the cost of transporting your elk back to your vehicle or to the processor in Craig. It doesn't include gratuities or the cost of your groceries for the hunt week.

You will not need a lot of fancy new gear. A high-powered hunting rifle with a scope that is zeroed and accurate at 200 yards is a must. Temperatures in the Colorado high country during October are extreme. It can be bone-chillingly cold or sunny and hot, all in the same twenty-four hours. Dress in layers and have a water bottle or two. If you are not in shape, start now by walking regularly and doing some cardiovascular exercises. The hills are steep in elk country, and the air will seem thin to Mainers used to breathing at sea level.

First Supper at Elk Camp. After a long day's hike up the mountain, my three elk-hunting companions gather around our makeshift table and make ready for the evening "meal." Pictured from left to right are Greg Goodman and Scotty Reynolds of Winterport and Pete Huston of Hampden.

What is the best hunt option, freelance or outfitter? A lot of that depends upon you and your budget. And of course, you can modify the aforementioned options, too. Frankly, there is an element of exploration built into the freelance option. I saw elk but never got a decent shot on my first freelance Colorado elk hunt. We had a memorable hunt, but we didn't see the elk in the numbers that we saw both years with an outfitter. Don't get me wrong: The Colorado national forests during October are full of freelance elk hunters who do bring home meat. Like most newcomer sportsmen to an area, though, the guided or semi-guided hunters generally fare better.

V. Paul Reynolds

Freelance Option: Hunting Elk the Hard Way

A few years ago I managed to carry close to fifty pounds of freeze-dried food and camping gear about three miles up a Colorado mountain at 9,000 feet. Then, three days later, I made the trip a couple of times up and down, carrying elk quarters and eventually my camping gear back to the truck.

I guess that qualifies me as a backpacker. Backpacking—real, big-load, calf-grinding pack-humping—is new to me. As a Boy Scout, I did the overnight down-by-the lake campouts, but for years, as an adult outdoorsman, I avoided the lure of the serious Appalachian Trail treks. In my mind, the discomfort factor trumped the romance of it all.

Then I began to notice the incredible improvements in backpacking gear: superlight one-man tents, feather-light sleeping bags, palatable freeze-dried foods, and relatively comfortable internal-frame backpacks. It dawned on me: "I can do this thing." If I could carry two days of camping gear on my back, new opportunities were presented for fishing and hunting!

In preparation for a Colorado backpacking elk hunt with my son and some younger men, I did a number of things. I bought a lot of new gear. A few overnight campouts were undertaken. These involved lugging my Colorado pack three or four miles to a trout pond and camping overnight. For six months, Diane and I walked three miles every morning. Some mornings I wore my new mountain boots and strapped on my 5,000-cubic-inch backpack full of firewood. (As you might guess, this lash-up drew some puzzled looks from neighbors.)

Of course, the Colorado mountains represented the Big Test! When you carry 25 to 30 percent of your own body weight up inclines in midday heat at higher elevations, you find out

Photo by Diane Reynolds

For any hunter, the bugle of an elk is a sound not soon forgotten. It alone, with or without a punched elk tag, is worth the price of admission. And a well-planned, backpacking hunt for cow elk done on public land is a lot less expensive than you might think! Read on.

quickly whether your carefully laid plans and physical conditioning were adequate.

Was I ready? Honestly?

The candid answer is: just barely. Although the Colorado mountains and hiking in thin air is not new to me, carrying that kind of weight uphill at altitude was a novel experience. Oh, I made it through. My younger hunting partners did not have to carry me or any part of my gear. My sixty-seven-year-old body panted and gasped for air like my English setter after a day of hunting thick bird covers on a hot day. There were an embarrassing number of water breaks along the way. At the three-mile mark just a few hundred yards from our destination, my legs "hit the wall." I said nothing to my forty-year-old hunt mates, but the old guy had come to the end of the trail for that day.

We had a great hunt, and the days got easier as our bodies adjusted to the altitude. My high-tech camping gear worked as advertised. We brought one quartered-up elk back down the mountain, and that was enough as far as I was concerned.

If you have thought about getting into the backpacking business, remember: There is a considerable amount of trial and error that goes with it. Don't tell my wife, but too much Reynolds money was squandered in the beginning on gear that was not satisfactory. So here are some pointers that might save you time, money, and physical discomfort:

- Buy the best gear first. (It makes all the difference in your comfort and safety.)
- Forget the external-frame backpacks. Purchase a big, high-quality, internal-frame backpack, and make sure that it is the right size for your particular torso. This is critical when it comes to getting the pack load on your hips, not your shoulders.
- Play around with freeze-dried foods. There is a world of difference; some are downright awful, and some taste pretty good when you are cold and famished.
- In your physical conditioning, work on those leg muscles. (I made the mistake of thinking that walking alone would prepare my leg muscles for load-bearing hikes. Not so in my case.)
- You cannot spend too much time winnowing down the size of your pack. You need to make hard choices about what is a must-have on the trail and what is not. Bill Irwin, who walked the entire Appalachian Trail (AT) without the benefit of eyesight, said that he started his trek with a 100-pound pack and was soon down to 35 pounds. He says that the ideal is to never carry more than 20 percent of your body weight in your backpack.

- One thing I did do right was to not make a purchase decision on my backpack and tent without thoroughly studying the options beforehand and talking to experienced hikers. I finally settled on a one-man mountain tent from Mountain Hardware and a Gregory internal-frame backpack (called a "Whitney") from L.L. Bean. This equipment was put through its paces in Colorado, and I couldn't be more pleased with it.

A side benefit of a backpacking elk hunt is that it's not nearly as tough on the pocketbook as hiring an outfitter to get you in and out of elk country. I have done these Colorado elk hunts the easy way and the hard way. Asked by my wife, who has been watching me "recover" from lost sleep and sore muscles, if I would do it again, I replied without hesitation, "Yes; it was the best hunting trip ever! The toughest, but the best."

Knowing what I know now, for your first elk hunt, I would encourage you (if you can afford it) to get hooked up with a reputable outfitter who can provide you with references. Short of that, I would get a small group of hunters whose companionship you enjoy and put together a freelance elk hunt to western Colorado. There is a wonderful national forest west of Glenwood Springs (be sure to make a pit stop there and soak in one of the natural hot springs). You'll be sharing a piece of history with one of America's most famous gunfighters, Doc Holliday, who lived out his quiet years in this small Colorado town.

By the way, the Colorado Rockies are spectacularly scenic in early October. The sound of a bugling bull elk against a backdrop of golden aspens, ragged green-black timber, and snow-capped peaks will make a lasting impression. However you choose to do it, the main thing is to do it! Go hunt some elk in the high country. You'll never regret it.

8

Slough Creek Shuffle

Rules and regulations. There's no escaping them, even in the great outdoors!

A few years ago, during an early-July fishing trip to Montana, three of us Easterners decided to do a three-day fishing and camping trek into the remote region of Upper Slough Creek in Yellowstone Park. The plan called for the three of us to hump our backpacks, fly rods, and gear far enough up the ever-popular Slough Creek to find some solitude, fishing space, and willing cutthroat trout. It's a hot, five-mile hike that is uphill a good part of the way, but well worth it once the panting and perspiration are behind you.

As it turned out, though, the toughest part of our Western fly-fishing odyssey was neither the hike up nor the hike back. It was overcoming the prerequisite pre-trip paperwork and maneuvering through the bureaucratic maze that park officials insist upon.

Photo by Diane Reynolds

The author plays a cutthroat trout near Third Meadow at Slough Creek.

Before you can backpack or camp overnight in remote areas of the park, you must first demonstrate a reasonable level of competence. This, presumably, was ascertained by a very young, semi-officious park ranger with whom I chatted, as I, spokesman for our trio, filled out all the paperwork. During the application process, we discussed length of stay, planned hiking route, age and relative health of hikers, the carry-in and carry-out ethic, outdoor experience of each applicant, and bears—grizzly bears. She and I talked a lot about grizzly bears.

Assuming that I'd measured up in the ranger's estimation, I signed the application and paid our Remote Camping Fee. To my utter surprise, she then informed me that the Remote Camping Permits are never issued on the same day that you apply.

"The rules require a two-day waiting period," she said with a warm smile.

"Wha?" I intoned with incredulity. "You mean, I gotta make the twenty-mile drive back here through the Pass again on Thursday?" (Our plan called for an early ascent up the creek on Friday morning, allowing us to beat most of the midday heat.)

"That's right," she said. "Those are the rules, sir, and I don't make them. You may pick up your permit any time after twelve noon on Thursday."

Then came the kicker. "By the way, you, as the leader of your hiking group, must also view a thirty-minute bear video before your permit can be issued. So I suggest that you come by my office no later than four p.m. This will allow time for the bear video. We close at five," she said.

Having a healthy respect for grizzlies, I understood why the park insisted that visitors and campers be educated about the perils posed by these big animals. So I told the ranger that I'd be back for my permit as instructed.

On the appointed day, Fred and I showed up at the ranger's office at about two p.m. to get our camping permit. No ranger. Her office door was locked. A note said: *Been called out. Back soon.*

We left and came back around four p.m. Still no ranger. At 4:45 p.m., I left the ranger a note.

We were here to pick up our permit and have been waiting most of the afternoon. Sorry that you were not here to show us the bear video, but I plan to stick to our timetable. We'll be heading up the creek at first light tomorrow morning, with or without the permit. I'm a woods-savvy Maine guide and very willing to give all bears a wide berth. We'll be careful. Don't worry.

Sincerely,
V. Paul Reynolds

Next morning, right on schedule, the three of us hiked the five miles to the Slough Creek's Upper Meadow. By ten a.m., we were setting up camp. The Montana sun was getting higher in the big sky, and the sage meadow that borders the meandering creek was heating up. But the trout were sipping surface stuff on the edge of the riffle, and, as I rigged my fly rod, I said to Fred, "And to think we've got this whole sweet place to ourselves!"

"I think you spoke too soon," Fred said, pointing across the meadow.

Sure enough, there was a lone hiker, head down and working his way through the sage straight at us, hell-bent for leather. It was a uniformed park ranger and he wasn't smiling. He was in a sweat. In fact, if he had been a Montana quarter horse, his flanks would have been lathered up good with white froth.

"Is there a Reynolds in your party?" he queried, a deep furrow in his perspiring brow.

"Ah, that would be me, sir," I said, trying to sound respectful but not cloyingly so.

The ranger then gave me a stern lecture about engaging in a remote campout without an authorized permit. I attempted to assert that there had been extenuating circumstances, but he wasn't buying. All he knew was that, damn it all, I had violated park rules by forging ahead with my plan without having seen the requisite bear video. And his boss, the young lady I had dealt with earlier in the week, had ordered him to walk ten miles in the midday Montana sun to deliver my permit and read me the riot act.

I apologized and nodded in the affirmative when he insisted that I stop in at park HQ upon my return and view the bear video. He then drank deeply from his backpack's hydration reservoir, offered us a cool "adios," and headed back down the trail.

Did I ever make it back to view the thirty-minute bear video? What do you think?

Part II:

Fishing

9

Into the Backing

In a lifetime of fishing, I have never been drawn to the dream of trophy fish. That is to say, big fish still impress me, but I'm not driven by the need to conquer big fish. I figure that if it happens, it happens.

In Alaska a few years ago, I caught a sixty-three-pound king salmon on the famous Kenai River. My guide broke his net getting that monster in the boat. Catching a fish like this is an experience not soon forgotten. Your arms get tired. And once a fish of this size is in the well and the photo is taken, you are slack-jawed by it all. Looking back, though, the fight itself was more akin to raising a fifty-gallon oil drum off the river bottom. A small land-locked salmon on a 5-weight rod put up a bigger tussle.

In fact, given a choice, I'd sooner catch a dozen small brookies on a #16 dry fly than one lunker brookie lured off the bottom by a bead head nymph.

The author (left) with an 18-pound pike caught on a fly rod on Labrador's Atikonak River. Guide Wilson Lawrence keeps the toothy critter at bay with the Boca grips.

What about you? We anglers seem to be of two different schools of endeavor: quality versus quantity.

Outdoor writer Lamar Underwood probably would roll his eyes at my attitude. "If you call yourself an angler," he would sneer, "and you profess not to care about big fish, it is just because you haven't caught many big fish." Underwood contends that all of us who fly-fish pray for that ultimate moment and the sound of a shrieking reel as a big fish takes out all our fly line and then tears into the backing. He writes: "Seen from a side angle, most fly reels offer a teasing partial view of the backing as it rests beneath the colorful coils of fly line. The tight band of braided line arouses deep and irresistible passions in the fly-fishing faithful. Here are 250 yards of emphatic reminder of the possibilities of sizzling big-fish runs that await the skillful angler."

Underwood may be right. Perhaps those of us who settle for small fish just need to have our appetites whetted. Honestly, now, how many times in all of your fly-fishing experiences have you had a fish take you into the backing? Unless you are a veteran Atlantic salmon angler or bonefish buff, your backing—like mine—only sees the light of day during periods of line dressing.

It's ironic, too, because most fly reels were made to sing. In all its years of holding line and backing for my Sage 9-weight rod, my old Medalist reel has wound down to the backing only twice. It saw action for the first time more than twenty years ago on New Brunswick's Upsalquitch River. An eighteen-pound Atlantic salmon sucked down my Rusty Rat and made a wild dash downriver with my fly line and most of the backing. "Chase the fish, b'y! Chase the fish!" yelled the guide.

Two decades later, that same old backing had a chance to unwind in the waters of Labrador's fabled Atikonak River. A world-class fly-fishing water for brookies and a variety of fish, large northern pike make for fast midday action on days when the trout aren't cooperating. Diane and I spent a memorable summer cooking and managing Matt Libby's Riverkeep Lodge on the Atikonak. A "working vacation," we managed to squeeze in some angling time in between camp chores.

At the suggestion of the camp's head guide, Wilson Lawrence, I used my lunch hour to cast big popping bugs over a so-called "p'yke hole" not far from the lodge. These big pike cruise the shallow river backwaters and like to hang out near the big rocks and overhanging arctic willows.

It was a still, bright day by Labrador standards. Even the incessant bugs were on lunch break. I eased the square-stern canoe onto a ledge island near the pike hole and began casting from shore. The big white popping bug made a couple of glubs as I stripped in line and then the water exploded. *Pow!* A toothy fourteen-pounder smashed the bug. Inexperienced in the aggressive ways of pike, I thought at first that a beaver or other large furbearer had grabbed my offering. But then I saw this fish's shark-like silhouette turn under the surface. The battle began.

In a matter of seconds, I was into the backing as the pike made a high-speed run for the open river. I laughed aloud and joyfully urged this fish on. In the next half-hour, three other large pike were hooked, beached, and released—with great caution. These predatory critters have toothy maws that can tear your flesh. Wire leaders and large pliers are a must for keeping the fish on and for releasing the fish safely.

Although pike fishing is sometimes a hard sell to the fly-fishing trout purists who come to Labrador in search of the trophy brookies, these shallow-water bushwhackers are fierce fighters on a fly rod. Pike also make fine table fare when filleted, chunked, and deep-fried in batter.

As Riverkeep Lodge's head guide Wilson Lawrence points out, pike are "nature's levelers," a balancing act that help keep the Atikonak watershed a fisherman's paradise that is home to trophy trout, salmon, lakers, and whitefish.

Last May, while planning my trip to Labrador and cleaning my fly reels, I had a premonition that the mothballed Medalist would get a long-awaited workout. Before leaving the Atikonak, I got into the backing one other time—on a big ol' brookie. But that's the subject of another fish story.

10

Snotty Trout

Among most self-respecting fly fishermen, the practice of
catch-and-release (C&R) has become the trout man's gospel, the
Holy Grail of trout angling. In Maine, for example, the careful
releasing of trout by conscientious anglers has become so fashion-
ably commonplace that, in some instances, fisheries biologists have
been forced to revise their trout-pond management strategies: A
pond can have too many trout! That's right; a pond with a limited
amount of feed can only support so many trout. To grow bigger
trout, you sometimes have to cull some of the smaller trout.

Proponents of the C&R ethic, especially the most pious,
argue that Maine could have Gold Medal trout waters just like
the famed Western rivers if only we Maine anglers would all
pledge never, ever to kill a trout. There is probably something
to this, but having recently returned from my fifth Western
fishing experience, there are some things—some unheralded

irregularities—about fishing those fabled catch-and-release waters of the West that don't get mentioned much in national angling magazines or on the Outdoor Channel.

Don't get me wrong; the West is a special place. Fly-fishing for cutthroat trout on a Montana creek in the shadow of the Beartooth Mountains is about as good as it gets. That's why I keep going back, and if you are a fly fisherman, you should find a way to get out there and soak it all up while you still can. Take out a second mortgage if you must; it'll be worth it.

I'm here to tell you, though, that there is a downside to C&R. To be more precise, there is a side effect to what I call institutionalized catch-and-release. We're talking heavily fished trout waters that have been designated C&R for many years— places like the Madison, Yellowstone River, Henry's Fork, etc.

Courtesy of V. Paul Reynolds

A bragging-size brookie, but back he goes after the photo opportunity.

On the popular Montana C&R river where Diane and I fish—
let's call it Cold Creek—the cutthroat trout are, according to the
fisheries biologists, caught seven to eight times in their lifetime.
So the bigger and older they get, the smarter they get. They
become tippet-shy, and many have a doctoral degree in drag-free
drift detection. My Montana-born friend Bruce Jensen, who lives
to fish, claims that the biggest cutthroats that hang out in the big
"sippy holes" are a little like animals in a petting zoo. When
you're lucky enough to get a hookup on one of these vermiculated
footballs, it knows from experience what the drill is. Rather than
fight for its life, Bruce contends, Old Walter plays it cool. He will
shake his head a couple of times as a way of saving face with his
fellow "cuts," and then simply lay back and await the obligatory
photo op near the creek bank followed by the ethical release.

In his book, *Fly-Fishin' Fool*, angling humorist James Babb
writes about his humiliation in trying to seduce these "snotty"
Western trout on "invisible flies." And snotty they are.

It takes Jobian patience to work these sophisticated lunkers.
On one section of Slough Creek, below the campground, there is
a big sippy hole where three-pound cutthroats fan lazily in the
back eddy, awaiting an easy meal. You can see them! But seeing
them and seducing them with an artificial offering are two different things. I rarely fish there. I head downriver where the
water moves faster in ripples and seams. The fish are smaller,
but in the faster water they will hit flies that you can see with
the naked, middle-aged eye.

Diane, on the other hand, spends her entire fishing day at
the sippy hole. In a morning, she will manage to get the best of
six or seven big "cuts." She does it with perseverance, patience,
and delicate presentations of light tippets and clipped-down,
barely visible dry flies. I have seen her outfish veteran trout men
who finally abandon the sippy hole in utter exasperation.

Snagging a bunch of big, beefy Montana cutthroats on small dry flies is pure angling joy, but I'd sooner catch a feisty Eastern brookie if given a choice. Compared with cutthroats, they possess a fighting will that is uniquely theirs. Babb calls it "bulldogging pugnacity." Out West you do have a choice, too. There are many ponds and creeks with holdover Eastern brookies from earlier stocking programs that predate the current Western fisheries doctrine, which is to one day have only native cutthroats in most Rocky Mountain waters!

In fact, my most memorable day this year out West was spent hiking and fishing—not for fat cutthroats, but for Eastern brookies at Grizzly Lake, which is not catch-and-release. When the wind drove us off the lake around mid-morning, we fished our way down the lake's outlet. From the relatively small brook, we caught, on a small Elkhair Caddis, some of the fattest and most strikingly beautiful twelve-inch Eastern brookies I have ever seen. My fishing companions Gifford Stevens, Frank Benn, and Danny LaBree and I fired up the backcountry stove and pan-fried a trout apiece.

What I have learned is that, like so many other serious avocations, the fly-fishing community has its denominational ranges. There are those who would rather take twenty lashes from Captain Bligh than deliberately kill a trout; conversely, there are others who always take home their limit. Catch-and-release is a landmark conservation movement that will ensure that others after us will enjoy the experiences we have enjoyed in hot pursuit of trout. But for me, an occasional wild trout cooked in a frying pan along a remote mountain stream is also an unforgettable outdoor experience.

11

Tippet Trickery

In his book *Practical Fishing Knots*, Lefty Kreh—America's high priest of fly fishing—writes: "An unwarranted mystique shrouds the simplicity of building tapered fly-fishing leaders." Lefty's probably right; far be it for any of us less-honed fly fishers to question the master. A down-to-earth guy, this is Lefty's way of saying that newcomers should not be intimidated. Fly fishing ain't rocket science, after all.

And yet so much of the fly-fishing sport is enshrined in mystiques, from waders and rod styles to fishing vests and the best sunglasses and brands of dry-fly floatant. Old-timers, who were casting artificials long before it became an outdoor vogue, scoff with contempt at the fancy gadgets and high-priced duds that have become the hallmark of fly angling.

Frankly, I love it all, the whole gamut. The endless gadgets, the new duds, the catalogs, the newcomers' cultist awe of the

Lefty Krehs, the old-time fly fisherman's stubborn allegiance to simplicity, the fashionable lady fishers in form-fitting waders, and the novices struggling with their timing. Most of all, I remain hooked on the rhythm and mystery of it, especially the utter unpredictability of trout. It is this mystery—this total uncertainty about why exactly a trout will strike a particular surface fly—that so intrigues me.

In fact, for me, the attempt to seduce a brook trout into gorging itself on a concoction of feathers and thread fashioned by my own hand brings to mind a certain adage: "The more you learn, the less you know."

Despite more than forty years of chasing trout with artificials and reading about the vast experiences of others more

Photo by V. Paul Reynolds

On Maine's fabled Grand Lake Stream, tippets matter. The author's son, Scotty Reynolds, seduced this reluctant salmon with a micro-size nymph and a delicate fluorocarbon tippet.

skilled at it than I, there is still not an artificial fly among my endless collection that is ever tied on my tippet with unshakable confidence. (Sometimes they all work, and sometimes, none of them work.) So I have begun to look beyond fly-angling ortho-doxy, which teaches that matching the hatch (the right fly) and proper presentation (smooth, ethereal delivery of the fly upon the water) is the thing. That is to say that if you have matched the hatch and made a good cast, and still the trout ignores your offerings, is there something else?

Oh, yes. Try tippet trickery.

A tippet, for the uninitiated, is that critical two-foot piece of monofilament at the end of a fly-fishing leader that attaches to the fly.

Fishing in the West two years ago over a creek holding but-terball cutthroat trout that were piled up like cordwood, I tried in vain for an hour to seduce one of those stream-sipping beau-ties with an array of flies and sizes. As a last desperate resort, I replaced a 4-pound tippet with a 1-pound tippet. Presto! The fish took. In a similar experience on a pond in Wyoming, a 1-pound tippet finally did the trick with big, stubborn rainbows that were surface-feeding. The catch-22 was that although I could coax a strike with the delicate tippet, the fish, once hooked, could not be turned without breaking off the tippet.

In early June of this year, while fishing a Maine trout pond with my two sons, trout were feeding on the surface at midday despite a bright sun and a flat calm. Yet nary a feeding trout would hit our mixed bag of offerings.

"Let's test my tippet theory," I suggested. "I'll put on a one-pound tippet and select a fly—any fly—at random from the fly box."

"Okay, Dad, show us your stuff," one of my boys said, humoring me.

With my skeptical fishing companions watching from their canoe, I made a short cast with a freshly installed 7.5X, 1-pound tippet. Attached to the delicate tippet was a small, greenish mayfly imitation randomly plucked from the old fly box.

Bang! A feisty fourteen-inch brookie, first cast.

So what made the difference—the tippet, or a lucky pick from the fly box? My "educated" guess is that feeding trout are not as discriminating about their diet as fly-fishing catalogs would have us believe. But they are fussy about the look of things—not so much color and shape, but the overall picture. I suspect that these trout will shy away no matter how well the artificial rides on the surface if they detect a curled tippet or a leader shadow near the fly. In the streams out West, where the average cutthroat has been caught and released at least seven times in a life span, the slightest drag ripple from a drifting surface fly will turn a trout away every time.

Of course, this is not news. Most fly fishermen learn sooner or later that improper leaders can spook a trout. My angler revelation is simply that for all these years, I've spent too much time fretting over fly selection and not enough energy and effort on the leader, especially the last two feet.

12

Best Nymph Patterns

Nothing in the outdoors quite compares with catching wild brook trout on a small dry fly. For me, sight-fishing—seeing the fish feeding on the surface and trying to place a #16 Adams softly on a "target riseform"—is an exciting challenge that never wears thin. The trouble is that conditions for fishing dries on top are not always right. Sometimes there is no hatch, or the wind makes casting difficult to impossible. When conditions don't cooperate, the angler has two choices: give it up, or get the artificials underwater and fish "wet."

Although it takes a lot to get me away from dry flies, I have witnessed over the years the effectiveness of fishing those bug imitations under the water. Truth be known, a lot more trophy brookies are taken on nymphs and wet flies than on well-dressed dry flies riding on the surface film.

If you are a newcomer to fly fishing, or if you are reluctant to fish "wet," I urge you to reconsider. As a stubborn dry-fly devotee over the years, I missed a lot of good trout action. Don't make the same mistake.

Granted, effective presentation of nymph patterns takes practice, and casting an awkward sinking line somehow lacks the restful rhythm of dry-fly casting. But one beefy brookie snagged on a nymph imitation can go a long way toward converting the dry-fly purist.

Enter Tom Fuller from Belchertown, Massachusetts. A national outdoor writer and encyclopedic fly fisher, Fuller has made a study of underwater trout flies. In fact, he has bared his soul and his savvy in a wonderful book, *Underwater Flies for Trout.* To help give us dry-fly purists a running start, Fuller lists his "core collection" of most effective subsurface mayflies. They are:

- **Gold-Ribbed Hare's Ear**
  According to Fuller, the "utility of this fly lies in its buginess." He advises you to carry an assortment in sizes 8 to 14. He believes that this fly imitates a Quill Gordon, a March Brown, and a Green Drake. This nymph pattern is also deadly when fished unweighted just under the surface as an emerger.

- **Hendrickson**
  Fuller says that this second in his choices of core patterns imitates a Black Quill, Mahogany Dun, and Sulphur Dun.

- **The "Generic"**
  This can be simply a smaller nymph in sizes 18 to 24 that has an olive-brown body and black wing cases. Examples of these would be a Pheasant Tail Nymph, an Olive-Brown Nymph, a Trico Nymph, etc. Fuller's book covers just about

Photo by V. Paul Reynolds

As any fly fisherman will tell you, nymph fishing requires oodles of patience and timing. My wife Diane tries her hand at "nymphing" from the bow of one of the famous Rangeley boats on the trout-rich Kennebago.

all aspects of pursuing trout with underwater flies. It is one of the most substantive and well-organized fly-fishing books I've yet to read.

If you're getting impatient waiting for warm weather and the hatches that follow, you might want to get serious about fishing "wet." Or, as Fuller puts it, "Isn't it about time you learned how to fish between hatches?"

13

Time on the Ice

New Englanders have come to expect cold weather in January, but the recent period of subzero temperatures and relentless high winds have given new meaning to the words *cold spell*. A rash of school cancellations in both Maine and Massachusetts, accompanied by alarmist weather forecasters who seem to take perverse delight in scaring older folks, makes some of us question whether New Englanders still deserve their national reputation for being stalwart, rugged individualists.

The New England Temperature Conversion Chart reminds us of our responsibility to live up to our legacy. Here's what the chart says about 10 degrees below zero: "Californians fly away to Mexico. All the people in Miami die. Even Toyotas won't start. Girl Scouts in Rhode Island are selling cookies door-to-door. Men in Massachusetts put the earflaps down on their hats.

Photo by V. Paul Reynolds

Maine ice fishing can be a special outdoor experience when conditions come along like this March day not far from Mount Katahdin. Dogs enjoy the action, too.

Mainers let the dog sleep indoors and put down their house windows before heading out to ice fish."

We never used to close schools during a cold snap. And youngsters of all ages used to walk to school, not ride a bus. Weather forecasters never told us it was "dangerous" to go outside on a bright, sunny winter's day.

It seems to me that Maine outdoorsmen aren't being as bold with the cold as they once were either. I have noticed that during November cold snaps, fewer and fewer deer hunters are standing vigil in the cedar swamps. Heater hunters are increasing in numbers. Sea-duck hunters are a dying breed. And more and more ice-fishermen are hunkering down at home in January and promising themselves a day on the ice in early March.

Maine weather can be fickle, with an endless capacity to delight and disappoint. It has taught me this: If I wait for the perfect weather window to hunt, fish, or camp, my outdoor experiences will be few and far between. So most of the time, I plan a trip and follow through come hell or high water. As a result, I have a pocketful of memories—some bad, but most of them good.

This past weekend as the deep freeze began to loosen its vise-like grip on Maine, my son, my grandson and his school buddy, my dog, and I snow-sledded into our northern Maine camp for a few days of ice-fishing. First day on the ice a fierce wind wailed down the lake out of the North. As we drilled ice holes and set our tip-ups, a wall of wind-driven snow moved down the frozen lake surface like a cloud of sea fog. Above the white layer, a bright sun and a cloudless, cobalt-blue sky served as a breathtaking backdrop to Maine's tallest mountain. Katahdin, bathed in pinks and purples, draws my attention almost as much as a sprung tip-up flag fluttering in the stiff wind.

For me there is a seductive grandeur to it all despite numb fingers and stinging cheeks. It is, well, *invigorating*, and it stirs your sense of adventure and heightens your awareness of His power to move the universe as He sees fit. We ice-fishermen are merely visitors here, outdoor voyeurs along for the ride.

The fish seem impervious to the wild weather scene topside. Our shiners are a major attraction wiggling beneath the ice. The pickerel, splake, and salmon bite like there is no tomorrow. That is ice-fishing, I have learned. Some days it is like watching paint dry; other days, like this one, it is nonstop action as tip-up after tip-up pops into view above the snowy windrows. The kids and the dog love it. It becomes a contest to be the first to see the flag, and the first to put a legal fish on the ice.

My grandson's friend, Nick, who is new to ice-fishing, learns fast for a thirteen-year-old. He is attentive to the flags and aggressive about his quarry in a quiet way. He bagged his first deer in November. A natural outdoorsman. He's hooked. The heritage will be safe with Nick.

Ice-fishing is one way to bring young people along. Dressed right and fed well, they don't seem to sweat the cold. As the wind builds at midday, the heated ice shack and its amenities become increasingly attractive. Among these are venison burgers, hot chili, and a game or two of cribbage.

By day's end, we are tired. The wind and the cold wears you down, even when there's lots of action. We pull our traps, collect our day's catch, warm our hands in the ice shack, and then head down the lake for camp. Young Nick has outfished us all, bringing home first fish, most fish, and biggest fish.

"If you don't want the pickerel, I'll take them," I say to Nick. Protective of his catch, Nick says, "Maybe." He says that he needs to check with his dad by cell phone to get his okay before parting with the pickerel.

Back at camp, the fires are stoked with dry beech. Outside it's twenty below zero, with a too-familiar north wind that is supposed to subside during the night. Inside there is a warming wood fire and scallop stew and biscuits on the table.

There will be more time on the ice tomorrow, and a forecast of light wind and moderating temperatures is music to our ears. Nick talks to his dad on the cell phone. We vote to turn in early.

"You can have my pickerel," Nick says, climbing into his sleeping bag.

14

Bigger, Better Brookies

If you survey Maine anglers to find out what coldwater species of fish they most enjoy pursuing, it's no contest. The beloved brook trout always wins, hands down! Those same anglers will tell you that they would like to see Maine grow more and bigger brookies. That angler sentiment was the impetus for Maine's Quality Fishing Initiative, a bold plan spearheaded by former Fish and Wildlife commissioner Ray "Bucky" Owen back in the mid-1990s.

Bucky's vision was predicated on the simple premise that if you put fish back in the water, they will live to grow bigger. It involved reduced bag limits and more-restrictive length limits. It has been about twenty years since the initiative was launched. Has it worked? The answer, if you ask serious anglers and fisheries people, is a qualified "yes." Although Maine's wild brook trout sport fishery seems to have made some positive strides, we still have a ways to go, and it may never again be like it once was.

Maine is blessed with hundreds of remote trout ponds that harbor big brookies. (See the list printed at the end of this book). Experienced trout chasers know that that there is a rule of thumb not to be ignored: the stricter the fishing regulations on a body of water the better the chances of snagging that speckled jaw dropper.

What is a trophy Maine trout, anyway? How big does a brookie have to be before we take special notice? Two pounds? Three pounds? More?

In his book *Big Trout*, author and angler Bernie Taylor says that a brookie must be four pounds or more to be worthy of the title "trophy fish." That may be a run-of-the-mill brookie in Labrador, but in Maine today, a four-pound brook trout is a fish to celebrate. In more than forty years of fly-fishing Maine waters, I've yet to boat a brookie in that class.

My friend, the late Millinocket guide Wiggie Robinson, has a pair of handsome trout in that class mounted on the wall of his West Branch camp. They were caught from a pond in Baxter State Park quite a few years ago in July, on a #14 Blue Dun. There was a green drake hatch on. A patient, persistent angler who was intimately familiar with a lot of Maine trout water, even Robinson wasn't catching trout of that size during his last few years.

You don't have to go back that far to pinpoint the halcyon days of Maine's trout fishing. In his book *Twelve Months in Maine*, the late Bud Leavitt wrote this in the mid-1970s: "Every year Maine trout fishermen grass a long line of three- to seven-pound beauties."

Other big brookie anglers of that era cited by Bud were John Dixon of Orrington, who boated a seven-pound, eight-ounce brook trout at Moosehead Lake. Patty Lou Walters of Waterville put a seven-pound brookie on the ice at Messalonskee Lake, and a Connecticut angler nailed a seven-pound, two-ounce trout at Pierce Pond in 1963.

Seven-pound Maine brookies! Just imagine. For a long time the Maine record brookie was an eight-pound, five-ounce brookie that guide Dixon Griffin took out of Pierce Pond in Somerset County. That record was eventually bested when an Aroostook County angler purportedly caught an even heftier trout—nearly nine pounds—at one of the Black Ponds. Legend has it that the angler actually dredged the monster brookie from a different pond altogether.

Fish stories, as we all know, can range from the evasive to the downright fictitious. According to a report from *The Maine Sportsman*, a new record brook trout was discovered belatedly. That publication reported that Mark Collins of Marshfield, Massachusetts, boated a nine-pound brookie at Square Pond in Aroostook County in May of 1997. That record has since been broken. In 2010, Patrick Coan caught a nine pound, two ounce brook trout at Mousam Lake.

Big Maine trout. Where do you get them and how? Although I am one of those easy-to-please fly fishermen who's content playing with ten-inch brookies on the surface with dainty dries, I did probe the big-trout question on your behalf. Here's what I found.

In his book *Fishing Maine*, author and angler Tom Seymour recommends Prestile Stream, Moose River, and Rangeley Lake for bigger-than-average trout. He also advises that big-trout shoppers carefully study the fishing law book. He writes: "Anglers intent upon taking trophy fish should take notice of those ponds that are strictly regulated as part of the Quality Fishing Initiative, because these will produce the largest trout."

Kennebec River outfitter and Maine angling advocate Bob Mallard has this advice for big trout chasers: "For rivers it is the Rapid River, bar none. The Roach sees some decent fish, as does the Magalloway. For large lakes, it is Eagle, but I believe we are hitting her way too hard in the winter to sustain the fishery. For small ponds, they are too delicate for me to mention "publicly," but Baxter and the AT are a good start. Access is key to the small ponds, and tough-to-reach ponds with strict regs are your absolute best bet (eliminate either, and the odds for big fish go way down)."

In *Big Trout*, Bernie Taylor coaches you not to overlook the obvious. Three of his big-trout lessons include:

- Successful fishing happens only when your fly is in the water.
- You can find success by eliminating the variables. Simplicity in your flies, gear, and techniques is the golden key to catching trout, especially large ones.
- If you fish in the places where the big fish are, when they are actively feeding, you will catch them.

15

Gifford's Little Secret

Now and then fishermen get excited about a fly that has been "out-lawed" in England or the Sahara Desert. That fly is said to be a wicked killer.
—*Arthur R. MacDougall Jr.*

Over the years, a lot of new streamer flies have been tied, tried, and talked about since famed Maine outdoorswoman Carrie Stevens first fashioned the Gray Ghost from some hat feathers. Most anglers have developed some strong prejudices about which streamer flies are the most effective. Generally these fly preferences are formed by experiences on the water.

A few years ago, I fished a number of small trout ponds in southern Aroostook County with Bradley angler Gifford Stevens. A hard-core angler and a fun guy to share a boat with, Stevens spent many hours fishing the County during his teaching days at

Photo by V. Paul Reynolds

Maine fishing guide Jeff LaBree created this very effective trout attractor he calls Jeff's Smelt. I can vouch for its usefulness, especially when trolled in trout terrain.

Houlton's Ricker College. He knows the waters. He knows his flies. And he loves to fish!

Although water temperatures were hovering just above 42 degrees, we managed to boat some trout. The biggest challenge was not catching fish. Keeping our body temperatures from dropping into a hypothermic zone made clothing choices as critical as fly selection.

Clothes that saved my life were: thermal underwear, cotton turtleneck, flannel shirt, wool jacket, hooded winter parka, double-layered wool stocking cap, and woolen gloves.

Flies that caught fish were: Black Ghost, Gray Ghost, Cecil Smelt, Joe's Smelt, Mickey Finn, and a relatively new creation, a Jeff's Smelt. Of this fly selection, the old standby Mickey Finn and the Jeff's Smelt saw the most action. While you probably have a few "Finns" in your fly book, it's doubtful that you own (or have ever heard of) a Jeff's Smelt.

Stevens swears by this particular streamer fly. His stepson, Jeff LaBree of Rockland, dreamed up this little beauty about eight years ago. Says Stevens, "I know of no pattern so effective for taking trout, salmon, and bass. It ought to be banned as a worm in a hatchery run."

After some coaxing, Stevens, with his stepson's consent, agreed to let me "share the wealth." Here's the recipe:

Jeff's Smelt

Hook:	Size 4 to 8, long shank streamer
Tail:	Bunch of golden pheasant tippets
Body:	Copper cord
Chin:	White marabou as long as shank, under which is yellow marabou one-half length of shank
Wing:	Light or dark marabou (gray); three or four strands of blue crystal flash; top with four or five strands of peacock herl
Head:	Red thread
Cheeks:	Red-dyed duck-breast feathers over which are two jungle cock eyes

Like most creative streamer flies, LaBree's concoction doesn't come easy. It involves some material and some labor. But it works, and surely will one day join the ranks of Maine's other legendary streamer flies. By the way, during the last week in April, Gifford Stevens boated three "board-size" brookies, a three-, four-, and eight-pound squaretail, all in one day on a Jeff's Smelt.

16

Pickerel Passion

They say first impressions are lasting. Not so, though, with fish. Take the chain pickerel. By rights I should loathe and fear this voracious, torpedo-like predator, but that's not the case; in fact, I love 'em! Let me explain.

I met my first pickerel as a four-year-old angler, and we didn't get off to a good start. My father introduced me to this toothy fish one overcast July afternoon at George's Pond near Franklin. To entertain me, while he was casting a plug for bass, Dad dropped my line on the bottom with a small yellow perch attached. Long story short: The Mother of All Chain Pickerel became impaled on my hook. We decided to keep the fish 'cause it was cheap groceries, and Dad had recently been put out of work. But when he attempted to boat this invader from the weeds, I screamed, so Dad elected to tow Jaws back to camp.

Photo by V. Paul Reynolds

If you like fish, don't pass up the toothy pickerel just because it has a lot of fine bones. Properly filleted, prepared and cooked, it can be exquiste table fare.

Time passed. I learned to love fishing for just about every fish Maine had to offer, save pickerel. Then I started taking my own four-year-old boy ice-fishing. To keep him interested after the hot dogs were gone, I began somewhat reluctantly to focus on pickerel. It worked. Scotty took to it. Together we raced from flag to flag. In fact, the fast action began to grow on us both, and my childhood pickerel aversion quickly faded.

The eating challenge remained, though. In our family, one never catches or kills anything that isn't consumed. And yet the Creator—it would seem—did not intend for man to feast on these bone-laden fishes. Those wispy, long bones have discouraged many a fish eater who decided that getting throat-speared by a sneaky fish bone was too big a price to pay for a mouthful of sweet meat. Nevertheless, through trial and error and with the help of some preparation tips from my Medford guide,

Doug Russell, we eventually adopted and fine-tuned a surefire way to cook and eat pickerel free of bone-choking anxiety.

Here's what you do:

- Take a sharp fillet knife and carefully slice off both fillets from the pickerel, leaving the skin attached to the meat.
- Scrape off the brunt of the larger scales (but don't work too hard at this).
- Turn the fillet over on a cutting board, meat side up. Using a razor-sharp fillet knife, start at one end of the fillet and draw the blade across the flesh until it reaches the underlying skin. Continue to make vertical cuts across the fillet. Space the cuts about a half-inch apart. Then turn the fillet and make a series of horizontal slices similarly spaced. What you are doing, in effect, is crisscrossing the cuts and making a cube steak of pickerel meat with the skin still attached and uncut.
- Place the cubed fillets in a refrigerator dish and pour over them a cup or so of evaporated milk. Let this set for an hour or so.
- Remove fillets from dish and roll in your favorite fish batter (a mixture of well-peppered flour and cornmeal will do fine).
- Place the battered fillets flesh side down in a skillet coated with a generous layer of cooking oil (olive oil is best), and cook until both sides are golden brown.
- Remove and drain well on paper towels. Serve hot.

Lot of work? Yep. But don't take shortcuts. The cubing, the milk-soaking, and the frying in hot oil all serve to minimize the bones and liberate all of that sweet, succulent fish flesh. And it is some good! In fact, prepared this way, a winter-caught chain pickerel will give any pan-fried trout or salmon a run for its money.

17

Trout Fodder

You wouldn't eat a red squirrel, right? A gray squirrel, maybe, but a red squirrel? No way.

One of my sons, when he was only a boy, reluctantly ate a small portion of fried squirrel. It was the penance he paid after dispatching the squirrel with his first BB gun. I'd warned him with the parental admonition, "You kill it, you eat it." This concept, handed down by my dad, is a good one. It teaches a young, aspiring hunter some sense of ethical accountability when it comes to the taking of an animal's life.

Of course, there are exceptions to the you-kill-it-you-eat-it-rule. There were a couple of nuisance critters around my place that, after having been dispatched, never made it to a Reynolds frying pan. Red squirrels for one. They can be pesky varmints that rampage birdfeeders and eat their way into homes and camps, looking for a free meal.

My friend, the late Wiggie Robinson, usually a gentle man, had it in big-time for red squirrels. They raised havoc with his camp and outbuildings along the West Branch of the Penobscot River. Every so often, the Millinocket guide would conduct a red squirrel "cleansing" around his place. But Wiggie saw to it that there was no wanton waste. After the deed was done, Wiggie, with appropriate reverence, ceremoniously placed the dead squirrels on the rocks alongside the river. A resident osprey became programmed to the routine squirrel sacrifice and swooped down often for a free meal on the Wigster.

A red squirrel met his demise at my hand a few weeks ago during a trout-fishing trip up north. My campmates and I did everything possible to discourage his midnight-snack visits to our camp kitchen. We smacked him with a broom. We threw a stick of wood at him. We set a rat trap baited with an exceptionally good sharp cheese. The crafty little bugger managed to eat all the cheese without tripping the trap. Twice he did that! After the second sleepless night, I did get lucky. The unwanted visitor got his when he least expected it, during the cocktail hour. Which isn't a bad way to go.

The squirrel's last move was a taunting, mocking pose atop the porch woodpile within arm's reach of me (thirty-five-inch sleeve). Ever so slowly, my toddy and a cheese and cracker were set aside. Then a lightning-fast tap on the squirrel's noggin with a piece of seasoned beech ended his camp-kitchen forays forever. But wait, it gets better.

You see, there was no wanton waste here, either. No, we didn't eat the little rascal; the trout did. Honest.

At this fishing camp where we had rented a cabin, the proprietor, over the years, has conducted a daily feeding of large "pet" brook trout. The big brookies hang close to the dock like drooling dogs awaiting a hambone. These slab-sided, hot-dog-fed

Illustration by Mark McCollough

"Big fish eat big bait" is a popular angler's axiom. On a whim I and a fishing buddy mused over whether a trout would tackle a small furry critter. We could not believe our eyes!

brookies look to be two to three pounds each, and, unlike their smaller, less-aggressive cousins, they know precisely when and where their next meal is coming from, and they're never late for dinner.

All of this got us to thinking: What would these rapacious dockside brookies do with an eight-ounce red squirrel? My fishing partner, Tom Fuller, who knows his trout, reminded us that big trout, really big trout, cannot survive on bugs alone. I'd heard that trout or bass had been known to pick off a mouse or a mole that found itself floating upon the pond. But a red squirrel? Only one way to find out.

So, in the name of science, we tossed the squirrel to the dockside brookies. With no hesitation, the largest fish there rose to the surface, snatched the squirrel, and then took its meal to the bottom. To our surprise there was no shark-like feeding frenzy, no ripping and tearing. The Boss Trout simply consumed the squirrel without fanfare—body, tail, and legs, gone.

Slack-jawed, we agreed: "You had to see it to believe it."

18

Parachute Adams and Buzzballs

Any fly fisherman worth his waders is always searching for that perfect fly, an artificial for all occasions. Once, when I was less exposed to the information overload that can overwhelm a novice fly angler today, I was a die-hard Hornberg man. Yes sir, trial-and-error fishing on a fair number of Maine trout ponds convinced me that a few Hornbergs was all a trout angler really needed in his bag of tricks.

A Hornberg was a multitasking artificial. Attach it to a sinking line and you could strip it through the water and snag brookies looking for small baitfish. If there was a green drake hatch on and a lot of surface action, you could wind-dry that big-winged jewel, drop it gently upon the surface film, and seduce a trout gulping those big drakes.

Back in the 1970s, while fishing for trout in the Colorado Rockies, my cowboy guide laughed mockingly when I tied on a

#12 Hornberg. "Ain't no self-respectin' cutthroat ever gonna bang thet feller," he said with a shake of his head and a spat of Red Man.

Needless to say, the Hornberg showed that cowboy a thing or two. Before the week was out, Sam offered to buy my Hornberg collection. I gave him one and kept the rest.

Since those "Hornberg Days," I have learned to be a little more flexible. After all, half the fun of fly fishing is dipping into those little plastic boxes and making a selection from a vast assortment of sizes, shapes, and colors, trying to "match the hatch."

I still have a special fly box, though, marked HORNBERGS, and they still work in spite of all the more-advanced fly designs that have been spawned by the fly-fishing craze. Be advised if you are a new fly fisher, or one prone to bowing to peer pressure: There are purists in the angling community who consider the conventional Hornberg to be the next thing to fishing with Garden Hackle.

"Hornbergs are too easy," one Maine outdoor writer once told me. "Hell, they should be outlawed as artificials unworthy of an angler concerned about fair chase."

I suspect that you—if you're a fly fisherman—have a favorite fly among your assortment of feathers and threads. Those of us who live to match the hatch are destined to be an insecure lot. Nature's capacity to produce an infinite variety of aquatic life forms always keeps us guessing, always apprehensive about whether we will be caught on the water without the right fly. It's what keeps fly shops in business.

The Hornberg, for all of its versatility, no longer reigns supreme in my fly box. It has been replaced in the hierarchy by another thoroughly commonplace artificial: the Adams. That's right. The Adams it is; to be more precise, the Parachute Adams.

During a recent ten-day fly-fishing vacation in trout-rich Montana, I had a chance to present flies to more good-size trout than I had ever imagined possible. Oh, other patterns worked. Yellow Humpies, Elkhair Caddis, Pale Morning Duns, Blue-Winged Olives. All of these caught fish when the size was right, but none, and no others tried, compared with the Parachute Adams when it came to a consistent attraction for cutthroat trout and brookies on the meandering creeks and mountain-fed streams of Big Sky Country.

In his book *The View from Rat Lake*, John Gierach writes: "Apparently, there are a number of very proficient, mostly local Henry's Fork fly fishers—born-again presentationists—who use nothing but the Adams dry fly in sizes 10 through 24 on all of the river's confusing hatches and who catch more fish than anyone has a right to."

It is no wonder that the Adams is the most popular dry fly in America today. With its mixed hackle and grizzly wings, this bug-like creation is both an imitator and an attractor fly. The fly was created by Len Halliday of Michigan, who used it on the Boardman River. Of the Adams, John Gierach writes: "It looks a little like everything, not exactly like anything, and seems to have great totemic power."

If you fly-fish moving water, the Parachute Adams, with its enhanced visibility, is a must for every fly box.

Building a Buzzball

Since this artificial trout fly received some notoriety in the *Northwoods Sporting Journal*, there have been a number of requests for its "recipe." The Buzzball has proven to be very effective most of the time. Of course, as Vermont fishing writer Tony Lolli says, "There are days when trout will hit anything, even a lug wrench." From all reports, though, the Buzzball is a trout fly that will earn its keep in your angling bag of tricks. Credit for disclosing this fly to me goes to tier Fred Hurley from Wayne, Maine. Here's how you assemble this little beauty, in Fred's own words:

> I came across this fly in *The Dry Fly: New Angles* by Gary LaFontaine, published in 1990. The Buzzball imitates a cluster of midges and is a very effective fly. On still waters it can be twitched along the surface to entice a strike. It is tied on a size 10–14 regular dry-fly hook and is made up of three dry-fly hackles (saddle hackles, because of their uniform barb length). All three hackles are tied in at the bend of the hook and each palmered down the hook shank, one at a time, from the bend in the hook to the eye.

> The first hackle is a blue dun which is a smaller size than normal for the hook size. This is followed by an orange hackle that is also smaller than normal and palmered through the first hackle. Lastly, a longer grizzly hackle is palmered through the other hackles. The top and bottom of the hackles are then V-clipped.

Photo by V. Paul Reynolds

A buzzball is a potent surface fly for trout. Created by Gary LaFontaine, it is said to impersonate a cluster of midges. If you don't have one in your fly box you are missing the boat.

19

Barbless-Hook Debate

All right, I confess: I used to be a trout hog. In the old days, you measured your success—your fishing prowess—by the day's catch. "I got my five; how about you?" was the fishermen's refrain. Today, there will be an occasional brookie taken home for my frying pan, but catch-and-release is the general rule. Certainly, the current-day C&R ethic has influenced my behavior on the water, but I think that passing of time has simply honed my appreciation and fondness for these marvelous wild fish.

One trendy trouter's totem that I have not totally embraced, though, is the venerated barbless-hook advisory. Yep, I know that among the fly-fishing community, barbless hooks are all the rage. A few years ago, while fishing with then Fish and Wildlife commissioner Bucky Owen, father of the Quality Fishing Initiative, I was gently admonished by him for not pinching off the barbs on my dry flies. Wherever fly fishermen go, they are bombarded with pleading reminders to go barbless.

Former Madison outfitter Bob Mallard was a die-hard barbless hook adherent, and required that all of his customers fished barbless on catch-and-release waters. Here is a sampling taken off the Internet:

- "Fishing barbless has become essential to the health of fishing stock. Pressure on fish stocks is growing intense as the popularity of fishing increases."
- "It's imperative that you use barbless hooks when practicing catch-and-release. As you can imagine, barbless fishing is less likely to injure fish, and will improve their survival rate."
- "Barbless fishing has its advantages: It enables you to release fish quicker, with less injury."

Photo by Paula Jensen

Although there is much to be said for the angler's catch-and-release ethic, fisheries biologists encourage the taking of fish in many Maine waters that just have too many.

But is it so? Will barbless fishing reduce fish injury and improve their survival rate? This refrain has been so oft-repeated in the fly-fishing community that it has become accepted as part of the Angler's Gospel.

It's been my belief that fish-release techniques are far more critical to fish survival than a barbed or unbarbed hook. From what I've seen, far too many anglers have yet to learn how to release a fish properly without touching it, or engaging in excessive handling.

This article from *Trout Magazine* by Robert J. Behnke claims that barbless fishing can actually be more damaging to released fish than fishing with the conventional barbed hooks:

> The fisheries research studies in Yellowstone Park have also helped to dispel some long-established beliefs.
>
> Contrary to popular opinion, it is not necessary to restrict catch-and-release fisheries to barbless flies only. A large proportion of Yellowstone anglers have only casual interest in fishing and are not highly skilled or experienced. Many use large treble-hook lures. The trout they catch are frequently left flopping on the bank while a camera is dug out and photos taken. Yet survival of the released trout is exceedingly high (99.7 percent) based on the 1981 study. Most all detailed comparative studies on hooking mortality have demonstrated no significant differences in mortality between trout caught on single, treble, barbed, or barbless hooks.
>
> There is, however a slight but consistent increase in mortality due to barbless hooks.
>
> John Deinstadi, a California Fish and Game Department biologist with long experience with catch-and-release fisheries, believes this is due to what he calls the "stiletto effect." Barbless hooks have the tendency to penetrate more deeply. Although mortality of released trout

rapidly increases with warmer water temperatures (especially as temperatures approach 70 degrees), under normal conditions, almost all mortality of trout caught on flies or artificial lures is due to rupture of the respiratory filaments of the gills or puncture of the carotid artery in the roof of the mouth. Because of their greater penetration power, barbless hooks are more prone to puncture the carotid artery. Large treble hooks often cause the least mortality because, unless the trout is quite large, the hooks cannot be engulfed into the mouth.

Jim Snowe, who knows angling and runs the fishing shop at Van Raymond's in Brewer, says that there is no big demand for barbless hooks or flies. Jim says, "I pinch down the barbs on all my flies. Not only does it make it easier to release the fish, but a barbless hook that gets embedded in my flesh is also a lot less painful to remove!"

Hmmm. Food for thought.

21

Green Drake Finale

A Hex—or, if your Latin is good, a *Hexagenia limbata*—is a bomber-size mayfly that shows up on Maine trout ponds in mid-summer, usually early July. For a trout, they are a turkey dinner with all the fixin's—a chance to get the most amount of food for the least amount of effort.

To a trout-loving fly fisherman, a Hex hatch is an adrenaline rush—a sight to behold. In fact, like a solar eclipse or an expanse of northern lights in the winter sky, a true Hex hatch on a trout pond counts as one of those special moments in nature. Truth is, my experience with Hex hatches can be counted on one hand. Still, one July Hex encounter stands out in my memory.

Diane and I were camped at one of Wiggie Robinson's favorite trout ponds in early July. The fishing had been slow all day. Then, just before dark, the Hexes began to bust through the still surface of the pond. Soon the pond was covered with these big-winged, lime-green duns. It looked like a flotilla of small sailboats "in irons," becalmed by the dying breeze.

Blup, blup, blup. The feeding began, and the pond was peppered with surface-feeding trout dimples wherever you looked. The trout gorged themselves for about an hour. They also took our big White Wulffs without hesitation. Then the Hexes disappeared as fast as they'd come on, and the fishing slowed accordingly.

There is an ongoing debate among Maine anglers about what to call these big bugs. Anglers who know a lot more about entomology than I do say that most of us misname the Hex, calling it a green drake, as in "Hey, Joe—you really missed it! As soon as the sun went behind the mountain, the pond was covered with green drakes. A wicked hatch! Never seen anything to beat it."

So the question is, I guess, "When is a green drake a green drake, and when is a Hex a Hex?" You don't care? Well, in that case, you're probably just a casual fly fisher of trout. Those of us whose heroes are fly-fishing entomologists like to really know our bugs, for that's how you get to know your trout and how best to seduce them.

I put the aforementioned question to Tom Fuller. Fuller, a seasoned fly fisher, outdoor writer, author, and aspiring entomologist, has written an informative book, *The Complete Guide to Eastern Hatches*. Fishing with Fuller is a learning experience. In late May, after getting skunked at one of my favorite trout ponds, we wound up throwing popping bugs at pickerel and crappies at Hermon Pond. Warm-water angling can be a nice change of pace for trout fanatics. The pressure is off and conversation comes easy. Here is his answer: "The differences between the eastern green drake (three tails on the dun) and the Hex hatch (two tails on the dun) are at best subtle. The eastern has mottled wings; the Hex doesn't have the mottling, but does have veins. Coloration and size really depend on the waters where they're found, and the fertility. The real difference is the double gills found on body segment #1 on the Hex. The eastern nymph has single gills on body segments 1 through 7."

As any angler will tell you, the Green Drake hatch is a happening. When these big mayflies do their thing and populate the surface water of a trout pond, it is a special moment for the fly fisherman.

As Fuller pointed out, when these big bugs are on the water, the fish are really fired up, and just about any big pattern will work. Wulffs, a large Adams, or a Hornberg never disappoint when the Hex hatch is on. Or, if you are lucky enough to be on the good side of Greenville's fisheries biologist, Tim Obrey, he may grace your fly box with a timely gift: a lethal fly he ties called a Sexy Hexy.

As always, the best of trout fishing in Maine begins to fade as summer comes on and water temperatures drive the brookies deep into the spring holes. But there is still time. The farther north in Maine you go, the more likely favorable water temperatures will hold a while longer. And who knows? You might get lucky and get in on a green drake hatch on a cloudy, humid day. You won't soon forget it, if it happens.

22

The Pink Job

The legend of the trout's sagacity . . . arises from man's conceit. If the trout can outwit us, the lords of creation, he must be superior to us in cunning.
—*P. B. M. Allan*

"You want to fish the dead water Friday," Gifford said. "I was thinkin' we could try that in the morning, and then maybe catch the evening rise on the river," he added as an enticement.

"Friday's good for me, Giff. Let's do it!" I said. One of my favorite fishing partners, Gifford Stevens of Bradley, is a skilled angler and a good man to share a canoe with anytime, even when the fishing is slow. He and I have fished most of Maine at one time or another. We have also shared campfires and remote cutthroat creeks in Montana and Wyoming. He always outfishes me at least two to one, all the while feigning humility, as if he didn't care who outfishes whom.

I know better.

Stevens is no slouch at the tying vise, either. As we were putting in at the dead water, he opened his fly box and handed me a couple of small pinkish streamer flies.

"Gee, thanks, Giff," I said. "Never saw any even similar to these. What do you call it?" I asked.

"No name as far as I know. A friend gave me one last year and it worked good on this water," he said.

Not to sound unappreciative, but it looked a little, well, *effeminate* to me, with its pink chenille body and gold ribbing. But I didn't say so to Gifford. In fact, I tied it on to my tippet as a gesture of appreciation for his thoughtfulness. I knew that if past was prologue, I'd snag the little, limp-wristed pink job on an alder bush by the third or fourth cast anyway. Then I'd tie on an old, staid, less-showy artificial—say, an Adams, or maybe a Goddard Caddis. Gifford would never have to know: dead-water diplomacy.

As we worked our way up the dead water, beyond the bony section of the stream, one thing became apparent. Our timing could not have been better. Although the water was a tad low for this time of year, the trout were making riseforms like this was to be their final meal before the winter set in. You guessed it. The trout fishing was exceptional! We released fifty or more trout and kept a couple for the pan.

Yes, and the little pink job with the fluorescent-thread head was deadly. And, contrary to conventional wisdom, there was a bright sun and no hatch that we could discern. Go figure.

That afternoon, we tried our luck on a well-known Aroostook river. Game warden Charles Brown told us that the river had been fished pretty hard during Memorial Day weekend, but that there ought to be a few good brookies in the deep holes.

By two p.m. there was a blinding mayfly hatch about as good as any we had ever seen on this particular stretch of water. Attached to the logs and sticks underwater were dozens of what looked to me like cased caddis. Considering the bug activity, fishing was

Photo by V. Paul Reynolds

When it comes to fly selection, a trout will fool or defy you every time. Seeing the Pink Job in Gifford Steven's fly book, I would not have given you a nickel for it. My mistake. It was deadly on Dudley Deadwater.

slow—at least for the first hour. A few hundred yards before our takeout spot we found, to our delight, a pod of good-size brookies feeding just under the surface.

For two hours we worked these fish with little success. Nothing interested them. Between us, we threw everything at them but Atlantic salmon flies. We tried #14 and #16 dry flies, small streamer flies, Copper Johns, Hare's Ear nymphs, stonefly imitations, Muddlers, Woolly Buggers, and the late Wiggie Robinson's first- and last-resort killer, the Maple Syrup. I even tried, in desperation, Alvin Theriault's fish-flavored version of the Maple Syrup.

What was going on beneath the surface? The answer eluded us. Even the Pink Job held no attraction for these fat brookies that shunned us with a vengeance.

We also wondered how, in the same day, two different trout waters not all that far apart could be so contrastingly hot and cold. What we experienced was all part of the intrigue and mystique of angling, why they call it *fishing* and not *catching*.

If you fish for trout, you know as well as we do that there *is* a fly that should have done the trick. Probably some type of an emerger. Darned if we could match it, though. What would you have done?

We quit for the day.

23

The Big Bug Battle

Zzzzzzzz . . . zzzzzzzzz. . . . swat. *Zzzzzzzz. . . .* swat. *Zzzzzzzz. . . .* swat.

That is not the sound of music. It is the sound often heard when a trout fisherman is trying to catch brook trout on an alder-choked stream or a big dead water. You know the drill. Brookies and bugs. *Salvelinus fontinalis* and the order Diptera. They seem to be inseparable. You can't have one without the other. It's the downside of good trout fishing.

Trouters all have their bug stories, too.

"Why, the blackflies were so thick they tried to carry off Uncle Herbie, and you know how big he is!" "You talk about bugs; man, they were so thick they blocked the sun and cast a shadow as big as a buffalo." "I'm telling you, they were so thick we were breathing them and gagging with the dry heaves. We

Battling the bugs at Upper Fowler Pond.

got some fir boughs and started a smudge fire right there in the cedar-strip canoe. I swear."

You haven't really experienced the bug terror unless you've fished Labrador in early July. One early evening on the Atikonak River, Diane and I were mesmerized by lunker brookies sipping surface bugs so close that they were slapping our waders. I was so concentrated on trying to seduce one of those slab-sided beauties that I actually forgot about the annoying cloud of blackflies feeding on my flesh. My fishing trance was broken only twice: once, when a stout (an eight-ounce Labrador horsefly) took a chunk out of my neck, and, again, when the stub of my smoldering cigar burned my lower lip.

Back at camp, under the gas light, Diane looked at me, aghast. "Check yourself out in the mirror," she said. My face was peppered with blotches of dried blood. I looked like an upland gunner who had spent a day hunting quail in the Texas sage with Dick Cheney.

Another time in late May during a particularly brutal bug season, Diane and I had an encounter of the bug kind on Little Houston Pond. It was a warm, windless morning. The trout were hitting good and the blackflies were as thick as I have ever known. As I chain-smoked cigars, Diane donned her bug jacket. Though the bugs could not reach her flesh, they began to work on her psyche.

"I can't take much more of this," she said with a wifely urgency.

"Golly, hon," I said, "the fishing is just getting good. You'll get used to the buggers. It's mind over matter."

As I recall, she was a good sport and finally resorted to a cigar.

Speaking of bug repellents, have you found one that really works? When I was a kid, my dad used to slather me with an utterly foul-smelling bug dope. It was, I believe, called Old Woodsman, and it was ranker than its namesake could ever have been under the worst conditions. It helped. As far as I can tell, modern bug repellents stopped working when the manufacturers watered down the ratio of DEET. The so-called homemade remedies don't work any better than the store-bought fly dopes, either. Writer Henry Beard has a very good definition of insect repellent in his book, *Fishing*: "One of a number of gag items available in the novelty sections of tackle shops, along with waterproof clothing, damp-proof matches, and long-life batteries."

Let's face it: You can't battle the bugs without using something that works. And for it to work, it's probably going to have to be nearly as bad for you as it is for the bugs. DEET works, but as far as I know, the commercial repellent makers are, for health reasons, not allowed to spike their bug potion with a big-enough percentage to do much good.

During my bug-battling trouting career, I have found only two ways to keep these nattering nasty nits at a tolerable distance.

1. Cigars
2. ThermaCELL

My doctor tells me that cigars are bad for me and to avoid them at all costs. (He is probably not a trout man.) As for the ThermaCELL device, it also comes with a precautionary statement: "Harmful if inhaled. Avoid breathing vapors." No wonder the bugs don't like it!

Of course, in a desperate buggy situation, in which your very sanity may be on the line, there is always the primitive bug repellent recommended by Maine survival writer Charlie Reitze. He simply finds a good low place in the woods and slathers his face, neck, and ears with black muck from the arboreal forest.

Zzzzzzzzz . . .

24

The Morning Rise

. . . fishermen value most the fish that are hard to take and value least those that are offered to everybody on a fishmonger's slab.
—*Arthur Ransome*

In the eat-or-be-eaten world of the animal kingdom, Mother Nature has equipped most prey animals with an immutable logic. A fish or a coyote, or any creature in between, learns not to expend more energy getting its food than the food is worth, nutrition-wise. The glaring exception to this law of nature is the foraging behavior of the complex, inscrutable bipod, *Homo sapiens*. Man.

It's as if man, once a primitive hunter-gatherer, lost his way in the march of progress. That's right. In his unchecked enthusiasm and unbridled passion for his pastime, the sportsman has been known to ignore the law of diminishing returns when it comes to fishing or hunting. And this is just the protein-in-versus-protein-out equation, with no factoring in the costs of fly rods, rifles, and big four-wheel-drive pickups.

Case in point:

"Wanna go fishing?" Bob asked me the other day.

"Sure thing. What's the deal?" I asked my friend.

"We'll just do the morning rise—have you back home by lunchtime," Bob assured me.

Now, I like to fish with Bob, and rarely turn down an invite. There are a number of reasons. Good-humored and easy-going, Bob is pleasant company in a canoe. A devoted trout man who has written a wonderful book about fly-fishing Maine's trout waters, Bob is also knowledgeable. We always catch fish. He knows some good places, obscure trout pockets, spring-fed streams that will give up a few trout even in warm weather. Like me, Bob is not averse to killing a few brookies for the pan either.

"Good. Be at the house by seven a.m. You might want to bring your seven-weight rod, too," Bob advised. "There's some nice trout there, and I've had trouble turning them when they get into the weeds," he said with a cocked eyebrow.

He also advised that I would not need my customary hip waders—that I wouldn't even need to get out of the canoe.

"You got a small crosscut saw?" Bob asked.

I did, and agreed to bring the saw without giving it a thought. Little did I know.

"What's the saw for, Bob?" I asked later, as he and I "geared up" the canoe and began sliding it down the steep railroad bed to the stream.

"Well, it's a little tangled with beaver dams and overhanging trees before we get to the spring holes. We may have to cut a branch or two," he said.

Photo by Diane Reynolds

My son Scotty and I catching the morning salmon rise at our favorite hole on the West Branch of the Penobscot River. This river, along with Grand Lake Stream in Washington County, are must-visit places for any fly fisherman who enjoys moving water.

After a few minutes on the stream, a few things became apparent. The water "was down some," as Bob put it. "We may have to drag the canoe some, too," he said. The beavers, in keeping with their reputation, had been busy. The eelgrass and water lilies were enjoying a banner growing year. In short, we faced some navigational challenges between us and the trout hole upstream.

The first hurdle was a large tree that lay across the stream, blocking our passage. Hence the crosscut saw. Since Bob was the stern man, I was to become the cutter. Standing in stream muck up to my knees, sawing away, it hit me. "What's this 'we' stuff?" I asked.

Bob was right about the low water and the need, in many places, to drag the canoe across stream grass and beaver debris. Knowing that Bob had a bum knee and was facing surgery that fall, I figured that he had no place dragging a canoe and fighting the stream muck. So I dragged him and the canoe like Humphrey Bogart in *African Queen*. (I'd say that Bob outweighed Katharine Hepburn by a good fifty pounds.)

Finally, we got to the trout hole. Bob was right. The trout, some decent fish, were hungry and cooperative. We caught a bunch on hoppers and muddlers. Some were kept for the pan. A fast, short strip of the line was the key. It all reminded me once again that in Maine, contrary to popular wisdom, you can catch brook trout all summer. The trick is to know the water and concentrate on the spring holes.

By noon, "we" were dragging the canoe and the gear up the steep railroad bed and then heading home with our limit of brookies. It was a good morning rise in spite of the obstacles. Of course, lesser creatures, looking for a nutritional return on their investment, would have avoided this protein quest as a losing proposition.

But then fish and coyotes don't care about the compensatory, soulful residuals, do they? The deepening of friendships, the lasting memories, and the good night's sleep.

No doubt, we'll turn around and do it all again next year. Anything for a couple of nine-inch brookies.

Part III:

Hunting

Hunting Tips

Deer

- Scout early and obtain landowner permission when possible.
- Look for deer in wet areas along streams, swamps, and lakes during hot, dry weather.
- Hunt during midday; big bucks often move at this time.
- Look for the most nutritious foods currently available in your hunting area. Deer will be nearby.
- When you locate doe and fawn family groups, bucks will be there too, anytime in November.

Grouse

- Hunt old apple orchards.
- If you don't have a dog, walk quietly in grouse cover and pause frequently.

Courtesy of V. Paul Reynolds

A good dog, a good companion and a good bird cover can leave lasting memories. Jay Robinson (right) and I (left) share the moment of a downed bird with his English Pointer.

Turkey

- Preseason scouting is the single most important part of turkey hunting. Scout several different areas to lessen your chances of conflict with other hunters.
- Practice your turkey calling diligently.
- Pattern your shotgun on a life-size target to know your effective killing range.
- Plan to hunt on weekdays, if possible, rather than Saturdays. Hunting pressure is lighter during the week, reducing chances for conflicts with other hunters.
- Be patient; with a four-week season, there is plenty of time. Birds are still active at the end of May, and there's less hunting pressure at that time.
- If bow hunting, use a string-tracker to aid in retrieving crippled birds.
- Be patient when calling: Give each setup thirty to forty-five minutes, as birds sometimes come in silently, especially in areas that have heavy hunting pressure.
- Do not walk in on another hunter who is "working" a bird. Repeated gobbling is often a sign of a hunter working a bird. Attempting to stalk the "gobbler" is not only dangerous, but it also interferes with the caller.
- Do not wear any clothing with the colors red, white, or blue. These are the same colors as a gobbler's head, and may draw fire from a careless hunter.

Moose

- Prior to the moose season, sight in your rifle.
- Moose often appear closer than they are, because of their large size. Keep this in consideration when estimating the distance to the moose before you shoot.
- A .30-30 can be used for shooting a moose, but it doesn't have the range of larger guns. A larger-caliber gun (.308, .30-06, 7 or 8 mm) may improve your success and reduce the possibility of wounding a moose.
- Be prepared to get your moose out of the woods. Rope, come-alongs, pulleys, a chain saw, and waders can be indispensable on your hunt.
- Respect other hunters and the nonhunting public by keeping your distance from other hunters; not blocking roads; and not hunting on well-traveled roads, near camps, recreation areas, and popular moose-watching areas.
- Remember: On most woods roads, log trucks have the right of way. Don't park your vehicle where it will interfere with log hauling.
- Quartering your moose will make it easier to haul and will reduce the risk of your meat spoiling.
- Skinning your moose, or filling the chest cavity with ice, will also reduce the risk of your meat spoiling.

25

The Black-Powder Option

While buying some percussion caps this week for my Thompson Scout muzzleloader at a local sporting-goods store, I couldn't help but eavesdrop on a conversation between a store clerk and a customer. The customer appeared to be a seasoned deer hunter who was a babe in the woods when it came to primitive guns. A well-intentioned young clerk was going through the fundamentals of black-powder guns with the customer.

"Tell me again, now," the customer said. "I will need a primer, a powder charge, and a projectile, right?"

"Uh-huh," said the clerk. "And of course there are different options, ya know? You can buy a gun that fires a percussion cap on an outside hammer, or you can go with what is called an in-line gun." He went on to explain the difference between an in-line gun and all the rest.

Black-powder option: Tools of the trade.

The clerk then gestured to a prominently displayed in-line muzzleloader. For a little under $300, the store offered a sort of "starter kit" for the new black-powder hobbyist. The kit provided the aspiring black-powder hunter with just about everything but a jack fir and a whitetail deer—the gun, the wads, the bore cleaner, bore lube, some .50-caliber balls, a primer dispenser, a powder dispenser, a rod rammer, a ball-pulling auger screw, a nice necessities bag, and an instruction book (in three languages, no doubt).

"Great," the man said. "What else will I need to get started?"

"Just a box of primers and some powder, and you're in business," said the clerk.

The customer didn't have a clue. His innocence tempted me to add my two cents' worth and put words to my thoughts: "Hmm, let's see now. You'll need a boy to carry your black-powder accessories, and a small dozer to get the new gun out of the blister pack. Oh, yes, bring along some plastic baggies to cover your barrel and percussion cap. And a sharp knife to cut through the gun smoke can be helpful, especially if you like to see the target after you fire . . ."

But life has taught me things. I've learned to control my mouth, and speak when invited to do so.

"How messy is this black-powder stuff?" the customer asked the clerk with a slightly furrowed brow.

The clerk looked skyward, as if carefully weighing that question. "Well, er . . ."

"Very messy," I broke in uninvited, and added, "Don't kid yourself—black powder is dirty and smelly!" In fact, most meticulous muzzleloader users bathe their gun barrels in scalding hot water more often than they do themselves.

The clerk looked mildly annoyed, but forced a smile. The customer seemed pleased that I had joined the conversation, which only emboldened me to step into the conversational circle.

"What about reliability?" the customer asked.

"If you keep your powder dry and your gun clean, these inlines will perform with dependability and accuracy," the clerk avowed with a straight face.

With raised eyebrows, as if waiting for affirmation from a neutral party, the customer turned to me. I told him my black-powder buck story, the one about the fat, little corn-fed Maryland buck that stood and looked at me after my muzzleloader misfired. (Nobody, including the author of the three-language instruction book, has ever advised that it's good practice to *always* fire two or three percussion caps through your gun before frontloading the powder and ball.)

As the clerk and customer discussed the various projectile choices that face a smoke-pole shooter (that's jargon for muzzleloader), I got to thinking about my confusion over projectiles. Although conventional wisdom teaches that sabot bullets shoot more accurately than the old-fashioned steel balls, my Thompson Scout seems to shoot better with a ball than a plastic-jacketed sabot slug. I decided it best not to add to the customer's already overloaded circuits by introducing this little trajectory tidbit.

Heck, Ray Hamilton over in Livermore, who wrote the book on black-powder hunting, has been known to experiment with grapeshot in his primitive guns.

The customer was not cowed by my observations or the store's vast array of choices. He bought the gun. We chatted on the way to our trucks. He confessed that he was about to join the ranks of the black-powder community for much the same reason that I did a number of years back: He didn't get his deer in November.

For all the folderol that goes with the black-powder option, I felt happy for this new Maine muzzleloader user. He has joined the ranks of nearly eleven thousand other December deer hunters who have extended their hunt opportunity for another few weeks.

As he drove off, I wondered if he was aware that a $13 muzzleloader stamp is required on his hunting license. I should have told him.

26

Gemstone Abby

For upland bird hunters, especially those with dogs that hunt, October is the month of months. Out in the covers, amid the alders and poplar groves, the sumac and mountain ash berries, men and women with whistles and high hopes will work their wonderful dogs. They will call, coax, coerce, and cuddle these tightly wound canid creatures with two-syllable names like Sadie, Dixie, Maxie, and Otto. At the end of the day, spent, mud-covered dogs will be watered, fed, and kenneled up. A few birds will be dressed. And then tired but happy hunters will relive the whole day, and talk—usually about dogs.

They do it for the dogs, you know. That's right. Most upland hunters do it not for the meat, but for the dogs: the English setters and pointers, the springers, the Brittanys, and the German shorthairs. As a lifelong meat hunter who has taken up with a bird dog late in life, I, too, am heading for the bird covers with Sally, a whistle, and high hopes.

Sally of Seboeis, my supple little eighteen-month-old English setter, is as ready for the hunt as I can get her. We've put in our training time, her and me. We've had a legion of help and counsel from experienced dog handlers such as Ed Brooks of Brooks Ridge Kennels in Newburgh, Wiggie Robinson of Millinocket, Steve Forrest from Hampden, New Brunswick Guide Doug Hawkes, friend Ron Hastie of Longmeadow, Massachusetts, and a word of advice even from flushing dog expert Jo Ann Moody of Waldo.

Here are ten things I've learned from the professionals who have patiently helped me and Sally through Bird Dogs 101:

- Keep it simple, stupid.
- Repetition and short training sessions are key.
- Dogs have good days and bad days, too.
- Start a dog from puppyhood and forge a bond. A "bonded dog" that wants to please will compensate for a multitude of training sins.
- If properly understood and responsibly used, electronic training collars can be humane and very useful.
- So much of what bird dogs do in the field is natural. As a novice trainer, I at times have been unwittingly the greatest barrier to my dog's learning curve.
- There are almost as many different theories about training gun dogs as there are dog trainers.
- A whistle will save your vocal cords.
- Bells are no good on windy days. There's no romance in beeper collars, but they do the job.
- Learn to laugh when dogs, birds, and shotguns don't do what you will them to do.

In New Brunswick, dog handlers often recount the legend of an English pointer named Gemstone Abby. On a windy, late-October day, Gemstone Abby locked up on a bird at four p.m. Her handlers tried in vain in the dark to locate her. Giving up the search, the handler returned at daybreak to find his famous dog after a few inches of snow had fallen during the night. At sunup, they found Gemstone

Photo by Fred Hurley

Sally on point. The author's English setter "cut her teeth" as a gun dog on pheasant at a shooting preserve in eastern New Brunswick.

Abby still on point. And there were no tracks around her in the snow. True story, they swear.

Now get out there in the briars and the brambles, all you upland hunters, and make the most of Maine's finest month. May the memory of Gemstone Abby be an inspiration to you and your best bird dog.

27

Deer Camp Pilgrimage

What is it about deer camps?

In my book *A Maine Deer Hunter's Logbook*, there's a chapter that delves into the mystique and special attraction that all deer camps have for hunters:

> Deer camps have always been special to me, as they are for most hunters. We may not take the time to reflect on just why these cabins in the woods hold a special place in our hearts, but we are subconsciously mindful of it just the same. A deer-hunting group that I have belonged to for close to forty years, the Skulkers of Seboeis, has had a number of deer camps over the years. In the early years, it was just us, a group of young men who shared a common passion: deer hunting. Today, our sons, the second generation, are Skulkers. This fall during our customary "work weekend," when we cut wood and perform a general fix-up in

preparation for the Big Week in November, a few prospective third-generation Skulkers were on hand. These young boys, you can tell, can't wait for the day when they, too, can settle in for a week at deer camp. And it won't be long.

Yes, what is it about deer camps? The march of time inspires us to ask these questions, and, as a writer, I have also learned that if you dig deep enough, you will always find other writers with a surer pen, and a better facility to capture the true essence of a feeling. Outdoor writer Mel Ellis wrote this about his deer camp:

> Even before I cross the threshold I felt at peace with myself and the world. I literally could heave a great sigh as though a burden of physical proportions had been lifted from my back. That was the kind of camp it was, a place that shuts out the world and all the worry that goes with it. It stood in good deer country, but I am sure it would have been the same under the sun of the Sahara or within reach of high tide. This camp was 5-pound chunks of American, Swiss and cheddar cheese standing on the cutting board, beans browned with sugar and covered with salt pork waiting on the stove. It was rifles standing in a corner, red clothing steaming on chair backs, tiny streams of water running across the floor from boots by the door, gloves drying in an open oven. There was frost creeping up the windowpane, snow piling high around the woodpile, tracks up the trail sifting full and fading.

Down East fishing guide Randy Spencer, a deer hunter, too, writes thoughtfully about deer camp in his book, *Where Cool Waters Flow*:

The arrival of each hunter to this annual summit is a jubilant, raucous affair. When all of us do finally arrive— some fatter, some thinner, some balder, some grayer, all older—we're each a sight for sore eyes, and say so. Convening here marks the passage of another year, and very few stones in that year will be left unturned during the full-voiced, nightly banters to come.

By the time you read this, I and some of my closest friends will be settled in at our deer camp for a week of hunting and good times. Most of my contemporaries, like me, have been making this annual November pilgrimage for close to fifty years! Imagine, a half-century. What I find most incredible, if not downright inexplicable, is that my ardor for the hunt and a

Photo by V. Paul Reynolds

First deer camp at Pearl Pond of Ebeemee was owned and operated by the Skulkers of Seboeis. The camp burned down in the early '80s and was never rebuilt.

137

week at deer camp has not waned with age. I expected that it would, but it has not. The prospect of a week at deer camp still excites and sparks an inner joy for me, even after all these years.

If you are a novice deer hunter, or an old-timer who has yet to spend time at a deer camp, find yourself a palace in the popple, as poet George Augustus Bixby called it.

Palace in the Popple

It's a smokey raunchy boar's nest,
with an unswept drafty floor,
And pillow ticking curtains,
with knife scars on the floor.

The smell of a pine knot fire,
from a stovepipe that's come loose,
Mingles sweetly with the bootgrease,
and the Copenhagen snoose.

There are workworn .30-30s
with battered steel stocks,
And drying lines of longjohns,
and of steaming pungent socks.

There's a table for the Bloody Four,
and their game of two-card draw,
And there's deep and dreamless sleeping,
on bunkticks filled with straw.

Ed and Lawrence, by the stove,
their gun talk loud and hot,
And Rob, has drawn a pair of kings,
and raking in the pot.

V. Paul Reynolds

Harvey's drafted again as cook,
he's peeling spuds for stew,
While Gus wanders in baggy pants,
reciting Dan McGrew.

Nowhere on earth is fire so warm,
nor coffee so infernal,
Or whiskers stiff or jokes so rich
nor hope blooms so eternal.

A man can live for a solid week,
in the same old underbritches,
He can walk like a man, spit where he wants,
and scratch himself where he itches.

I tell you, boys, there's no place else
where I'd rather be come fall,
Where I eat like a bear and sing like a wolf,
And feel like I'm bull pine tall.

In that raunchy cabin out in the bush,
in the land of the raven 'n loon,
With a tracking snow lying new to the ground,
at the end of the rutting moon.

—George Augustus (Gus) Bixby (c. 1905)

28

Daybreak in Vermont

My introduction to rural northern Vermont did not start well. It had snowed hard. My son and I had shoveled out the driveway of his newly purchased home in the hill country. Driving my truck out onto the main road, I drove up the hill and backed into my son's neighbor's driveway in an attempt to turn around.

The neighbor, whose reputation preceded him and whose name I already knew, was waving frantically at me from his woodshed. I stopped the truck, rolled down the window, and turned off the heater fan so that I could decipher this man's shouts.

"Get off my land," the man with the white beard ordered. "You have no right to turn around in my driveway." His big German shepherd growled as if to punctuate his master's ire.

Not wanting to make matters worse for my son's neighborhood relations, I assumed an apologetic air. "I'm sorry, sir, I meant no—"

He didn't let up. I began to get hot under the collar.

"What's your name?" I asked in a low voice, with a glare and a scowl.

"Ricker. Larry Ricker," he replied with a little less gusto.

"Oh, I know you. You're the plowman around these parts. Any chance of you plowing my son's driveway?" I asked.

The conversation became less heated. Before the day was out, we talked hunting, horses, and why so many of Mr. Ricker's neighbors have big white letters painted on their cow barns that read TAKE BACK VERMONT. He plowed my son's driveway at no charge. In kind of a tacit apology, he, a native Vermonter, explained how carpetbaggers from other states were moving in and trying to change them and their state in ways they didn't appreciate.

My introduction to this flinty Vermonter left me a little wary of introductory meetings with other white-bearded men in flannel shirts working manure spreaders behind dairy farms. Wanting to hunt Vermont turkeys near their back forties, however, I knew that I would simply have to work at winning them over.

During four days of turkey hunting I got to know some of these hardworking rural Vermont folks and their land. I liked what I saw. No, it was more than that. I discovered for myself a new-old frontier and was smitten by it.

The first morning of our hunt, Diane and I awoke at four a.m. to three inches of fresh snow. Not an ideal day to hunt longbeards, but we did see some hens and tried unsuccessfully to lure a jake across a field in a spitting snow.

During the week we saw a dozen or so lone hens feeding in green fields along edges of hardwoods, but the males—wherever they were—were not in a talking mood. The last morning, while walking a power line, I held an abbreviated conversation with a distant tom, but he was not interested in coming closer to check out the source of the "sexy" purrs.

In Vermont, all you need is the price of a license to hunt turkeys. Unlike Maine, there is no permit drawing, and you can kill two birds. Everybody hunts, and on Sunday, too. Although I met a local hunter who did bag two jakes in one morning, most hunters I talked with were finding uncooperative gobblers who just weren't in a talking mood. And, as one hunter told me, "If they won't talk, you can't find them."

I came back to Maine without a Vermont turkey, but I did bring back a bigger prize: a discovery that the Green Mountain State is a spectacularly scenic and topographically unpredictable place that gets under your skin. My previous exposure to Vermont had been superficial. A wedding in Rutland. A day of fishing on a famous trout stream. A visit to a maple syrup farm.

There are two Vermonts, I suspect, just as there are two Maines. A woman I know said that she was attracted to Vermont because it was a "politically progressive state run by intellectual liberals." That's the part of the Green Mountain State that never held much attraction for me, and apparently the same holds true for those white-bearded cattlemen in their flannel shirts who paint signs on their barns.

The Vermont I got to know was the one I beheld at daybreak. Hunkered down in a turkey blind, I sat reverently as the morning sun cascaded across the endless rolling green hayfields and hardwooded hilltops. The lime-green buds of new growth contrasted sharply with darker-green hemlock boughs that held up remnants of snow from the night before. Small birds sang. Roosters crowed. Among the distant hills, lights twinkled back at me from hillside homes as residents started their day.

At midday, driving the incredible network of winding, unpaved back roads looking for hunt options, I saw modest homes nestled in the hilly backcountry. There were some places that bespoke outright poverty and a hardscrabble existence, but always, the scenery and breathtaking vistas.

Above all else, these northern Vermonters, whatever their politics and wariness of strangers, are people of the land, even today. It seems to me that this is more true for northern Vermont residents than other rural New Englanders. Gardens are being turned over virtually everywhere you look. Chickens run loose. There are hog pens in the most unlikely settings. Even the smallest homes are raising a beef critter or two out back. Working dairy farms dominate the landscape almost as much as the spiraling hills and deep valleys.

If the TAKE BACK VERMONT signs mean what I think they mean, it is easy to appreciate the rural Vermonter's sense of the land and suspicion of outsiders. Cynics, or Vermont's transplanted "urban" progressives, may toss their proverbial noses in the air, sniff, and say that more needs to be done to help these folks and enrich their lives.

What a fool thing that would be.

29

The Goodman Elk

Greg Goodman wanted an elk so bad he could taste it.

During his first elk hunt in Colorado, three years ago, the Winterport man, who held a cow tag, watched in awe as a large-racked bull elk stood within shooting range. He watched the bull through the scope on his Winchester .300 Magnum rifle. In the crisp Colorado mountain air, vapor wafted from the bull's nostrils as it made its way across the open drainage. Steam ascended above the big animal's backside.

Goodman put the scope crosshairs on the bull's front shoulder. In his mind's eye, he could feel the trigger squeeze followed by the solid kick of the gun against his shoulder. At about a hundred yards, it would have been a high-percentage shot—especially during that heart-pounding moment when the bull stopped, rolled his head back, and bugled.

Courtesy of V. Paul Reynolds

Greg Goodman.

But Goodman, like the other three hunters in his group, didn't have a bull tag. When you go on a low-budget Colorado "meat hunt" for elk, you go the cow route. A cow tag is half the price of a bull tag. But there is no charge for watching one of these Rocky Mountain monarchs strut his stuff. There is a thrill in just the seeing, and useful story material for that night's campfire chat with the rest of the crew.

That same year Goodman did see two cow elk, but they were at distances he considered marginal for his shooting ability. He declined the shots. Elk were taken that year, however, by his hunting companions.

Two years ago, under tough hunting conditions, Goodman was the only hunter in his group of four Mainers who even saw a legal elk. Still-hunting the dark timber late in the afternoon on the last day, two cow elk trotted through an aspen grove at about forty yards.

"I rushed the shot," Goodman remembers. "Never touched the elk," he admits.

This year, year three, Goodman wanted an elk worse than ever. His hankering deepened when the other hunters in his group had filled their cow tags by sundown on the first day. He had spent an entire day hunkered down near an elk crossing in a big drainage. Save for a cold wind from the northwest, nothing much else happened. That night, as his fellow hunters celebrated the filling of two cow tags by roasting a slab of backstrap over some hot coals, Goodman fell into an introspective funk.

Seeing his preoccupation, his companions encouraged him to abandon the easy hunt in the drainage and still-hunt the elk in the dark timber high above their campsite.

The next morning Goodman was up early. His campmates wished him luck from the warmth of their sleeping bags. In the starlight, he worked his way up through the steep aspen groves toward the dark timber that spreads out 1,500 feet above the drainage. It is a tortuous climb, and even the best-conditioned hunter must stop every few minutes to slow his heartbeat and gasp in the thin air. Goodman, a quietly determined man in his early fifties, was in the mood to push himself this day. He reached the dark timber just as light was breaking in the east and, to his delight, beneath his boots there was a tracking snow!

A novice Maine deer hunter, Goodman nonetheless sensed right off that he had hit pay dirt. The dark timber, with its big lodgepole pines, firs, and tangle of bleached, gray blowdowns, had that "elky" feel to it. He thought that he could smell the elk. His instincts were soon confirmed by multiple elk tracks; some seemed as fresh as his own. He checked the direction of the breeze that was beginning to stir with the advancing day and began a slow, methodical pursuit along what appeared to be a fresh cow elk track.

Courtesy of V. Paul Reynolds

Greg Goodman (foreground) and his hunting buddies drag his first elk down the mountain in western Colorado.

As he recalls, Goodman had been on the track about twenty minutes or so. Suddenly, there it was! A big cow elk with head down, feeding at about thirty yards. "I could have hit her with my bow," Goodman would later recall. "All those practice shots at two and three hundred yards. This wasn't what I had expected," he said.

Goodman's .300 Magnum barked one time and the 400-pound elk dropped where it stood.

With an elk down and not a lot of experience field-dressing a big-game animal, Goodman then tried to reach the rest of his crew on his handheld radio. Unable to reach his buddies, who were busy in their own right, packing elk meat down the same mountain from yesterday's hunt, Goodman, resigned to his fate, rolled up his sleeves, honed his knife, and went to work.

Within an hour, Goodman had his animal quartered. As instructed, he piled boughs and snow over the four elk quarters, attached a piece of his clothing to one of the quarters, and urinated near the meat cache. (This seems to work in keeping scent-sensitive wolves and coyotes at bay, at least for one night.) He then rolled up the forty pounds of backstrap, placed the meat in his daypack, and began his triumphant trek back to camp. Before departing, he marked his kill site with his GPS and got out his orange tagging tape to flag his backtrack as he worked his way down the hill.

Before that day was over, Goodman and his crew would exchange celebratory hugs and verbal exultations. Then they would all make that breath-busting journey up the hill, retrieve the Goodman elk, and carry and drag the quarters back to camp.

As you might guess, Goodman, the "successful" elk hunter, earned himself a wonderful outdoor memory that day on the hill in the dark timber. Only those who have been there, who have shared the magnificent long views of snowcapped peaks and endless layers of golden aspens shimmering against spiraling, blackish-green conifers, can fully understand the intensity and totality of the experience. Goodman now knows. What he may not know—because for some reason, these things often go unsaid among fellow hunters—is that in the eyes of his hunting companions, he did indeed rise to the occasion. Not merely because he had killed an elk, but because he did it right in every way.

Goodman, because of his determination and persistence, killed an elk after three years of effort. Best of all, he did it in a way that brought credit to himself as an outdoorsman and to all who call themselves hunters.

30

Running Shots

If they are being honest, most veteran deer hunters will admit to having taken a shot at a full-out running deer. As a young deer hunter, I took my share of low-percentage shots. A couple of deer in bounding flight did fall to my snap shots. Looking back, however, I feel no particular soul-satisfying sense of pride in those kills. It was luck, not skill as an outdoorsman or as a marksman. Without doubt, a few deer ended up wounded in my haste to put meat on the table at the expense of good sportsmanship.

What about you? As a deer hunter, where do you fall in the running-shot debate? Some of you will dismiss out of hand my view that low-percentage running shots at deer are impractical and push the margins of fair chase. Legendary trophy buck hunters, the Benoits of Vermont, have made the running shot almost a deer-hunting standard in their deer-hunting videos.

Illustration by John Ford

Hunters differ in their views about the ethical aspect of running shots at deer. I no longer take those low percentage shots, but I confess that I once did.

And they would have the right to cross-examine my case by asking, "Well, how many trophy bucks have *you* bagged in your fifty years in the deer woods?"

"None," I would respond.

Then, smugly, they could reply, "We rest our case!"

R. G. Bernier is another well-known trophy whitetail hunter. In his book, *The Deer Trackers*, he never really delves into the fair-chase implications of the running shot. In one of his chapters, "Tools of the Trade," he does explain that his choice of sight on his Remington .30-06 pump is a William's peep sight equipped with a twilight aperture. He writes, "I have always shot with a screw-in aperture and it has never prevented me from being able to locate running game."

So it follows then, that Bernier, like the Benoits, has no misgivings about taking the running shot. Putting yourself in their shoes, or boots, it would be difficult to resist a running shot at a fleeing trophy buck, especially if you had been on the track all day and darkness was coming on.

T. S. Van Dyke, an American hunter/naturalist on a par with conservationist Aldo Leopold, wrote the classic, blue-chip deer book, *The Still-Hunter*. He didn't have much use for the running shot. He writes, "*Bang! bang! bang!* goes your rifle again, and still the brown goes on. Stop. Save your cartridges. He is wounded, and if you empty your rifle-magazine he may get out of this ravine before you can load again. It is evident that you are now too excited to hit anything; and therefore you had better take a few moments' time to cool down. And in the meanwhile fill up the magazine of your rifle, for you may need all the shots it will hold."

Of course, each and every deer encounter, by a deer hunter, is unique, with its own set of circumstances and split-second decision-making. There are running shots, and then there are running shots. A so-called "Texas heart shot," taken at the rear end of an exiting deer, is just plain wrong and unethical, period. On the other hand, a deer at thirty yards, moving at a fast walk sideways through open hardwoods, may present a decent target if the hunter can pull ahead, hold on an opening, and wait for fur in the scope.

As hunting ethicist Jim Posewitz writes, "The most important measure of hunting success is how you feel about yourself." This is where ethics and the ethical hunt come in. It is said that ethics is how you behave alone in the field. It is what you do, or don't do, when no one is watching. It is between you and your conscience.

Van Dyke, who was a frontier judge when he wasn't deer-hunting, or writing about it, expresses a belief in *The Still-Hunter* that is no less relevant to whitetail hunters today than it was in 1923.

31

High-Country Hunt

It was October in Western Colorado's high country. The air was clear, dry, and thin. Golden aspen, snowcapped peaks, and ragged skylines of black timber made for spectacular scenery. The elk, as we learned the day before from glassing a beaver pond from a high spot near our spike camp, were plentiful. That same day, late in the afternoon, we had watched a ten-point bull elk munching grass in a meadow not far from camp.

That was yesterday. This is today. It is the opener of Colorado's first rifle season for elk.

By four a.m. the tent woodstove is helping to ward off the mountain chill at 11,000 feet. Hunters quietly dress and ready their daypacks. There is anticipation in the wispy air. It blends perfectly with the smell of perking coffee and bacon in the pan. The four of us, Eastern deer hunters all, are about as charged up for a big-game hunt as we have ever been. After a year of planning, this is the day it could all come together.

"I'm psyched," my wife Diane says as she and the rest of us—my son Scott, my son-in-law Jacques, and I—gather outside the outfitter's well-seasoned spike tent. Dawn is breaking to the east with a clarity that is memorable. A bull elk bugles his presence not far off. It is a scene that seems almost choreographed, like a sequence from the Outdoor Channel.

With looks at each other, we silently acknowledge the special moment. Then, the hunt is on. We separate and head out, each hunter intent on following his hunting instinct and personal vision. Jacques strikes out for his makeshift tree stand overlooking a sweeping meadow not far from our tent site. Diane takes a position in the aspen overlooking a narrow funnel that leads to the beaver pond below camp. Scott works his way down the big slope behind Jacques amid the giant aspens.

Although this is an unguided hunt, outfitter Adam Moore's advice echos in my ears: "Find a place overlooking open places and stay put. You don't need to walk yourself to death or thrash about in the tall timber. Be patient. Those elk will come to you."

Still, I can't help myself. The tall timber beckons me like a seductress pursing her lips. Despite Adam's counsel, I tiptoe into the tall timber on little cat feet. "This feels right," I tell myself. "I'll keep a low profile, Adam. Honest. I will steal silently in, find a place on a game trail in this tall timber, and stay put."

Less than thirty yards into the timber, I hear the elk coming. Suddenly, there they are! My heart pounds. Down on one knee, I shoulder the .270 and try to find a target in the 4-power scope. There is a small herd of elk of every size and description close aboard and trotting from left to right through the big trees. Caught by surprise, I am too overwhelmed to select a respectable cow and take my shot. The whole scene reminds me of my first duck hunt. Too many targets! "You can't shoot 'em all," my veteran waterfowling companion had said. "Pick one, and go for it."

The elk disappear and things get quiet again. I suck in a lungful of air and scold myself gently for not keeping a cooler head. I sit tight, sipping water. Soon the gunshots of elk hunters echo off the craggy mountain faces that loom above the tree line. Minutes pass, and then, again, the elk are back. The duck shoot repeats itself, though the trotting elk are farther away this time. Just as I am about to squeeze off a shot at a passing animal's forward shoulder, I see a big rack of antlers and catch myself in time. Then the animals are out of sight. I take another scolding, less gently this time.

More shots from the meadows down below. Perhaps my hunting companions are more adept at animal identification than I?

"This is a strange problem to have," I tell myself. "Too many animals. This is the unexpected." I decide that patience is needed—that as the hunting pressure builds and the day warms, the elk will begin to disperse amid the sheltered timber and work their way in small groups up my way.

As pledged, I find a small, grassy opening among the mature spruce and lodgepole pines and hunker down in the shadows for the rest of the morning. Just before noon, on cue, a large cow elk steps into the grassy opening behind me and hesitates long enough for one eighty-yard shot. The .270 shatters the solitude and puts the animal down for good. My hunt is over. For the next two hours, I field-dress my kill and quarter it. As instructed, I put the elk quarters in cloth game bags and cover them with fir boughs. They will be picked up tomorrow and packed on mules for the twelve-mile trip back to the outfitter's base camp in the Routt National Forest.

By two o'clock the stillness returns to the mountains. After a sandwich and some tea, I lash the forty-pound elk backstrap to

Photo by V. Paul Reynolds

A real cowboy! Our friend, Colorado wrangler and elk guide Richard Kendall helped us and showed us the ropes in the high-country hunts. An expert marksman, Kendall has taken many elk and trophy mule deer.

my pack frame and head back to camp. Walking through the aspen groves and up the lung-busting slopes, I feel bushed. The ascent and the weight of the elk loins slow me down. No matter. Each rest stop is a chance not only to catch a breath, but to drink in the ceaseless splendor that is autumn in the Rockies. The whole experience washes over me like a baptismal bath. I make a promise. "You'll be back to do this again, while you still can."

Before our hunt was over, our outfitters packed out four elk from our camp—one taken by each of us. They were pleased with our hunt, and made the comment that Eastern deer hunters tend to do quite well hunting elk in the high country. Much of our time in the mountains was spent not hunting, but hiking, climbing, picture-taking, scouting, splitting firewood, and just kicking back and soaking it all in.

32

Lost in the Woods

During November, before the deer-hunting season con-
cludes, at least one deer hunter will not find his way out of the
woods before dark. It happens without fail, and, if past is prologue, usually there will be more than one lost hunter. Some live
to tell their story; others have not been so lucky. Historically,
those hunters who perished did so because, in their panic, they
could not keep their wits about them. They were not prepared.

During last December's black-powder season, a hunter in
western Maine became hopelessly lost in snowy conditions. He
wandered aimlessly. He fell through the ice. He became hypothermic. He did not know how to use his GPS properly. In short, he
was a textbook example of how not to survive. Yet by sheer good
luck, a snowmobiler happened upon him in the nick of time.

In reality, none of us possesses a true sense of direction.
Under the right circumstances, the most seasoned woodsman

can get lost. The difference between spending an uncomfortably long night in the woods and dying from dehydration and exposure usually boils down to attitude and fire-making capabilities.

Maine survivalist Charlie Reitze, who writes the "Outdoor Survival Tips" column for the *Northwoods Sporting Journal*, says that he always finds himself worrying this time of year about who the next lost hunter will be, and how that hunter will deal with his plight. Like most of us, Reitze has been "turned around" a few times in the woods as darkness came on, and is familiar with the dreaded feeling of panic that tries to get its vise-like grip on the lost hunter.

Charlie's advice:

If you get lost, admit it to yourself. Sit down and force yourself to think.

1. The first five minutes will be spent thinking about how to keep yourself from bolting—from being your own worst enemy.
2. Once you have conquered those first five forest-goblin, lunatic minutes, you've made it.
3. The time can then (and will) be spent on constructive thinking:
   a. Draw diagrams.
   b. Think of major road directions.
   c. Are you going up a mountain or down a mountain?
   d. Have you crossed a mountain already?
   e. Were there any logging roads?
   f. Mark well your present location and use it as a base.
   g. Break off branches.
   h. Notice landmarks.

If it's an hour before dark, accept your plight. Get a fire started and prepare a shelter. Don't sweat! Keep yourself up off the ground. Leaves, even wet leaves, are a great insulator. Stuff leaves between your body and your outer clothing.

Photo by V. Paul Reynolds

There is no night longer than one spent lost and alone in the Maine woods. Dawn is a welcome sight.

The next decision can be a critical one with consequences: stay put or try to find a way out? Search and rescue doctrine from the Maine warden service is unambiguous—"Stay where you are. We will find you."

Much has been written about what to do if you are lost in the woods. Given today's sophisticated navigational technology, and the search and rescue skills of the Maine Warden Service, staying put when you are hopelessly lost makes more sense than ever.

Of course, there are exceptions to every rule. If hypothermia is an issue, and there is no way to get a fire started, moving may be your only chance of survival. Most logging roads usually lead to travelled roads, but they can be tricky. The warden service is very good at what it does, expecially when it comes to finding missing people in the woods. Weather permitting, there will be warden aircraft looking for you not long after someone makes the 911 call. If you can get a fire going, and feed it lots of green boughs and thereby create signal smoke easily spotted from the air, the odds are astonishingly good that you will not have to spend another night in the woods, at least not alone. Most game wardens are pretty good company.

Of course, there are the time-tested cardinal basics that all hunters are taught by hunting safety instructors:

1. If you don't have a clue about your location, STAY WHERE YOU ARE! The Maine Warden Service is the best at finding lost persons. By air or on foot, using dogs or not, Maine game wardens will find you.
2. Get out in the open and keep a fire going.
3. Be prepared to fire three signal shots.
4. Above all else, make sure that your hunting survival kit contains a spare compass and multiple fire-starting methods (waterproof lighters, protected matches, and so forth). In addition, a small Ziploc bag of tinder could be a lifesaver on a dark, rainy night in the Maine woods.

33

Venison: Care and Cooking

A former career newspaperman, I've never been able to stop asking questions, especially of outdoor people who have a lot more experience than I. "What's the best deer gun, David? How do you bait your bear sites, Randy? When's the best time to make the Allagash trip, Gil?"

If I've learned anything from my constant quizzing of guides, outfitters, and assorted woods curmudgeons, it is this: Everybody has a different opinion! Sometimes this lack of consensus among respected outdoor people can be confusing to the novice out-doorsman looking for the last word on a perplexing question.

The proper care of wild meat is one of the areas that has had me wondering over the years. You hear so many different views. Take the aging process, for example. Our family has cut up and packaged more deer than I have bothered to count. Although we never deep-froze a deer we didn't like, some cuts of venison have been better than others. Some more tender; some more tasty.

And I've never known quite what to think about the advantages of aging wild meat. Knowing that domestic beef is aged at precise temperatures, I suspect there has to be something to it. But letting a deer hang in the barn for days with widely varying temperatures makes me nervous. So the Reynolds Rule of Thumb has been to skin the animal the first day and get it cut up and in the freezer by the following day.

One thing we have done is put a small amount of backstrap in an airtight Mason jar in the refrigerator, and it's always seemed a tad tastier by the second week. Once, while ice-fishing, I found the remnants of a coyote-killed deer on the ice. A piece of a hindquarter frozen in the snow (only thing left) was liberated and seared in a hot skillet over an open fire. Although this practice is frowned upon by game wardens, it was the only dinner I ever shared with a coyote. That venison was aged, teeth marks and all, and was the best I had ever eaten!

But this is all nonscientific, anecdotal stuff. After all these years of wondering about the true value of aging venison, I stumbled across something scientific—"empirical evidence," as the scientists say. Here it is, from a great book titled *Best Venison Ever*, by John O. Cartier:

Q. Is there any scientific evidence to prove that aging increases the tenderness of venison?

A. A study conducted by the food-technology department at Texas A & M University found that aging retards rigor mortis and extends it over a longer period of time. This process significantly increases the tenderness of venison taken from six study groups involving 30 whitetails. The research also found that aging increases the water-holding capacity of

venison and causes the breakdown of muscle fibers. Both
factors help increase tenderness. They prove without doubt
that aging definitely improves the quality of meat taken
from any given animal.

There it is. One more time: *The research also found that aging
increases the water-holding capacity of venison and causes the breakdown of muscle fibers.* You can take it to the bank. Cartier goes on
to point out that the best aging temperatures are from just
above freezing to 38 degrees. Minimum aging time is five days;
a week is best. Cartier ages his critter by quartering it and placing it in an old refrigerator for a week.

By the way, if you can find a copy, Cartier's book is an excellent, no-nonsense guide to preparing and cooking venison. It
contains recipes and insightful tips on caring for wild meat.

I feel sorry for folks who never get a chance to sample venison. Properly cared for and cooked, nothing—including a big,
juicy cut of prime beef—can compare with a serving of pan-
fried venison. As a matter of fact, not only is venison good, but
it's also good for you. Unlike corn-fed Western beef that is heavily marbled (full of fat), most venison is extremely lean, high in
protein, and low in fat.

As a young deer hunter, I discovered that there are almost as
many different views about cooking and caring for deer meat as
there are about hunting techniques. Some of the cooking and
caring tips that have been passed down from old-timers make
good outdoor lore, but just don't pass the straight-face test.
Here are two:

- Cook venison well-done. This will safeguard against brain-
  worm or Lyme disease should the deer be infected with ticks.

- Leave the hide on the hanging deer. It will enhance the aging process.

I know a fellow, an excellent hunter, who slices all of his deer meat, including tenderloins, razor-thin. Compounding this cardinal sin, he then fries his venison wafers until they look like beef jerky exhumed from an Egyptian burial site. Not good. We'll fry some the right way in a second.

As for hanging the deer, assuming that the outside temperatures are hovering near 40 degrees or below, it's best to get the hide off—the sooner the better. My Maryland friend, a professional cook who consistently produces incomparable cuts of venison, doesn't take chances with Maryland temperatures. He gets the skin off as soon as possible, quarters the animal, and ices down the meat in a big camp cooler. He then repacks the ice for about ten days, allowing the meat to age. And rather than slice his venison and pack in Ziploc bags for the freezer, he places the aged venison cuts in one-quart Mason jars and stores them in the fridge for up to three months. You get excellent aging of the meat this way.

Now for the best part: the cooking. This is tried and true. All of the wild-game recipes and marinades and assorted kitchen skullduggery cannot beat this simple, no-nonsense approach to venison preparation.

Cooking Venison and Venison Tea Gravy

Fetch your best cast-iron skillet (no Teflon jobbies). Crank the heat up and melt a small amount of butter in the skillet just before adding the meat. Drop in medium-thick slices of venison tenderloins. Salt and pepper. Cook for a minute on first side. At the same time, brew a half-cup of tea. Turn the venison cuts and sear on the other side for no more than an additional minute. (By now, if you're doing it right, there'll be some smokin' 'n' sizzlin'.) Remove meat and place it in a bowl (not a plate) and pour tea into hot skillet. Stir the tea around the hot pan and then pour the "tea gravy" onto the fried venison. The tea gravy recipe is courtesy of Dana Young.

As you savor the pan-fried venison, dip a biscuit into the tea gravy for an added treat.

34

The Real Trophy

When it comes to hunting and fishing, I have long felt that big isn't necessarily better. I know that this flies in the face of the popular outdoor TV programs, where trophy bucks and lunker rainbows are the main attraction. Not that I have anything against those who live to bag a twelve-pointer that dresses over two hundred pounds, or to outwit a gobbler with a ten-inch beard. I respect trophy hunters and appreciate the competitive spirit that drives them.

I guess we are all different.

On my "trophy wall" at home, there is a shoulder mount of an eight-point buck deer. It's not an ol' bruiser. In fact, it's a young buck with a small but pleasingly symmetrical rack. Outdoorsmen who visit my home take one look and I can tell what they are thinking: *Why would he go to the expense of mounting a small buck like that?* The answer I give to those bold enough to ask (or chide) me is, "Well, you had to be there, man. It was more the moment than the deer."

My son-in-law, a Florida conch from the Keys, was beside me that day, on his first Maine deer hunt. The deer bolted out of its bed near us and ran across the chopping full tilt. I yelled at him to stop. Damned if he didn't obey, stopping inches from the edge of the chopping and one leap to safety. His pause was a mistake. I dropped him in his tracks at 168 yards, a long standing shot for me. Frankly, I got lucky. Now, years later, when I glance at the young buck on my wall, the memory of the hunt comes flooding back. It is a sweet memory, and it gets sweeter with time.

Flash forward to a recent April, opening day of Maine's turkey season. I had been watching a respectable long-bearded gobbler out back, but decided not to hunt him. It seemed too easy. I'd save him for Diane who couldn't hunt until the following week. Shuffling out of the sack at 3:30 a.m., I ate a quick breakfast and drove to a spot I know. After a short walk in the fog, I found my old spot under a big pine tree alongside a large field and, after placing the decoys—three hens and a jake— about twenty yards from my ground blind, I hunkered down.

The field was shrouded in fog that seemed to thicken as daylight began breaking on the eastern horizon. The eerie stillness was at last broken by a distant gobble, then another. A couple of fly-down yelps from me brought a response from the tom, or at least it seemed to be answering my call off in the distance. This went on for half an hour. Decision time. Should I move his way and try to cut the distance, or stay put? Move, I guess. Underdressed as I was and fighting a chill, moving would be a welcome change. But an inner voice told me to tough it out, stay put. I did. Nothing; no sounds for about an hour. The fog began to lift and the sun worked its way above the hemlock trees behind me. I leaned back to soak up some warmth from the sun's rays.

It was then that I spotted some turkeys about three hundred yards away, on the far end of the field. A few hens, a couple of jakes, and one strutter doing his thing. He looked to be a mature tom. A couple of clucks and a purr from my slate call brought his head my way for an instant, but then he was back at the business at hand. I decided to wait it out and observe the proceedings. Soon, one by one, the hens worked their way back into the woods.

A couple of soft purrs. The strutter looked toward my decoys from across the field, and to my delight, began inching his way across the field toward the decoys. Halfway across the field, he—and the three jakes trailing him—came to a full stop, and like a chorus line, all froze in their tracks with their necks

Photo by V. Paul Reynolds

Game trophies mean different things to different people. Sometimes the memory of a hunt can be a bigger trophy than a set of big antlers. Watching this big gobbler strut his stuff at daybreak from a ground blind is a turkey hunter's golden moment.

extended and eyes looking straight at me. The jakes were in lockstep behind him. At thirty yards, it was obvious that this strutter was an elder jake. No beard that I could see, but a sizeable male turkey nonetheless. In full strut he followed the script, stopping beside the jake decoy, stretching his neck to the fullest, and talking up a storm.

To shoot or not to shoot. A second or two to decide. *Blam!* I put him down with my little Remington 20-gauge pump. A trophy hunter would have probably turned down the shot, waiting for a true long-beard. Not me. The setup was too good. The choreography and the orchestration were flawless. The crescendo in the turkey woods rose to a perfect pitch. The kettle drums rolled and the cymbals awaited to complete the metaphor. There had to be a shot. After all, killing a turkey is the name of the game. His sacrifice left me with a memorable hunt and a wonderful meal or two.

If you hunt, you know that there are hunts, and then there are hunts. Maybe I'm guilty of elitism or rationalizing, but that was the best turkey hunt I have ever had, and I've killed much bigger birds. Walking out of the woods that morning, I asked myself, "Why does this hunt seem so special, so gratifying to me anyway? After all, this jake slung over my shoulder is nothing to brag about."

The answer must have something to do with the verbiage in the *Gray's Sporting Journal* subscription ad: "When the quality of the time spent afield means more to you than what is brought home."

Don't get me wrong; I dig wild meat. But I guess I also hunt for the hunt, for the real trophy.

35

Diane's Deerburger Soup

Three of us got back to the campsite chilled to the bone. It was dark, and though the north wind had subsided, it wasn't getting any warmer. Casting a fly all day into that wind with cold fingers can give a fisherman an appetite. Lunch wasn't much.

We were hungry.

While my boys took care of the gear and kindled a fire, I fired up the propane stove and set a big saucepan of soup over the blue flame. Looking over my shoulder at the bubbling soup, I got the feeling that my two dinner companions had something a little more substantial in mind than a bowl of hot soup. But having sampled their mother's deerburger soup a few other times, I let the boys swap looks and said nothing.

They were in for a treat. Steaming bowls before us, we dug in. Soon the exclamations flowed. "Wow, Dad, this is some good! What's in this?"

Photo by V. Paul Reynolds

At elk camp in a tent in Colorado, Diane Reynolds prepares breakfast for her "boys."

In a few minutes, the three of us polished off a two-day supply of Diane's soup. Finally, with full bellies and warm souls, we sat by the crackling cedar fire and swapped stories.

As we climbed into our sleeping bags, one of the boys suggested that it might be a good idea to mass-produce Diane's Deerburger Soup and sell it at Doug's Shop 'n Save.

"Who's got the time," I mumbled, nearly asleep. "Too much fishing to do and too many columns to write . . ."

The next best thing to marketing Diane's Deerburger Soup at a supermarket is to simply share the recipe with other outdoor people. Keep in mind that in more than forty years of eating

174

wild food and writing about the outdoors, this is only the third recipe I have found worthy of my ink. Here it is:

Diane's Deerburger Soup

1 tablespoon olive oil
4 garlic cloves, minced
1 big onion, chopped
2 lbs. ground lean venison
half-can of beef broth, or 2 beef bouillon cubes
1 cup water
1 cup diced celery
1 to 2 cups diced carrots
corn cut from 4 frozen ears (or 1 can whole-kernel corn, drained)
4 to 5 whole frozen garden tomatoes (or 1 large can of whole tomatoes)
1 teaspoon Worcestershire sauce
bay leaf, basil, fresh-ground pepper, and salt, to taste
1 teaspoon sugar

To prepare, heat olive oil in a cast-iron pot. Add garlic, onion, and meat. Cook on low heat for a few minutes, until meat is browned and onion is transparent. Then add broth and water. (You might need to add more water later.) Add remainder of ingredients and simmer until carrots are tender.

Diane suggests experimenting with your favorite herbs. She believes that the herbs and veggies from the home garden and freezer really make the difference.

By the way, those other two noteworthy recipes are for North Woods Beans (pg. 180) and Venison Tea Gravy (pg. 166).

36

North Woods Beans

For me, one of the pleasures of outdoor cooking is discovering a new or better way to do things. Most of the time, the better way to do things is learned from others. Over the years, I've made it a point to watch experienced outdoor cooks, sample their culinary delights, ask lots of questions, and take notes. And I always try to give credit where credit is due. Venison Tea Gravy is an innovation I learned from former Hampden resident and friend, Dana Young, an outdoor cook whose kitchen creations at times rise to sheer artistry.

There is, though, one dish that I can take most of the credit for: North Woods Beans.

In my youth, beans and home-baked yeast rolls were a weekend ritual. I grew up with baked beans on Saturday night. And as a young man on my own, I was unwilling to settle for B&M, or any beans from a can. So I cooked baked beans. Lots of beans. I sampled the baked beans of others, and I experimented with my own beans over the years. In fact, if my bean pot were a used car, it would be on its third engine. It has seen a lot of miles. (My children and grandchildren find their way to our home on Saturday nights more than any other night of the week.)

To be blunt, the baked beans of others have not impressed me. Some are soupy and mediocre. Some are tasteless. Others are a dining experience akin to consuming a plate of molasses-coated bird shot.

So what follows is *the* baked-bean formula. North Woods Beans! The best you'll ever eat. Trust me on this:

North Woods Beans

On Friday night, soak 3 cups of yellow-eye dry beans in a bowl of water, overnight. On Saturday morning, drain beans in a colander and put them in a good, old-fashioned bean pot.

In a mixing bowl, combine the following ingredients:

1/4 cup of brown sugar

1/4 cup molasses

1 teaspoon salt (my wife uses less)

scant 1/2 teaspoon black pepper

2 heaping teaspoons dry mustard

Add to bowl lots of scalding hot water (4 to 5 cups) and stir the bean liquor well. Pour liquor over beans in the bean pot.

Add 1/8 to 1/4 of a stick of real butter, plus one strip of uncooked bacon cut up in short pieces.

Add a small onion, if you like. I've decided over the years that onion, while it adds some taste, is not worth the tradeoff—unless you live alone, or with an old dog who loves you unconditionally.

Place pot with tight cover in 300-degree oven and cook
for 5 to 6 hours (check water level every hour or so, keeping
beans covered with water at all times). Remove pot cover
during the last half-hour or so, to brown the beans.

Suggestion: For the ultimate North Woods dining
experience, serve beans with venison steaks, Bakewell
Cream biscuits or brown bread, coleslaw, beet pickles, and
cottage cheese.

Because my wife and I like to eat, cook, and hunt—and in
that order—a fair amount of our time is spent experimenting
with and reading about wild-game recipes. At one time or
another we have cooked and eaten just about every legal critter
that has either fur or scales.

Prepared and cooked right, most wild animals are nutritious
and tasty. I have been pleasantly surprised by muskrat pie and
frog legs. There are exceptions. Included among my short list of
not-so-pleasant expe-
riences with wild-
game cuisine have
been beaver burgers
and a turtle soup con-
jured up by Maine's
legendary outdoor
writer, the late Bud
Leavitt.

As with most fans
of wild meat, the
cloven-hooved critters
rate tops with us. You
just can't beat deer,
moose, and elk for fla-
vor and nutrition. We

Illustration by Tom Hennessey

*At the Reynolds house over the years, Satur-
day night is not Saturday night without a
big plate of homebaked beans, pan-fried
venison tenderloins and buttermilk biscuits.*

179

have learned over the years that properly aged and packaged meat is unbeatable. And, as for cooking it, simplicity is the key. A venison loin seared on a hot buttered iron skillet and served rare cannot be matched. If you ask me, there is not a marinade or a complicated recipe that can ever improve upon the untampered-with natural flavor of pan-fried venison.

In fact, a venison backstrap from a Maryland whitetail, properly aged and prepared by my hunting buddy and professional chef, Dana Young of Westminster, is a dining experience like no other. He insists that the secret is in the way the meat is aged, and there is no arguing with that kind of success.

Worth arguing about, though, is what I call "the great cover-up." In a past issue of *North American Bear* magazine, cooking writer Susan Kane pushed her Bear Roast with Bourbon Cream Sauce. It has a mouthwatering ring, right?

I'm skeptical. Not counting the four-pound bear roast, she lists seventeen additional ingredients, not the least of which are two tablespoons of rosemary, half a bottle of red wine, half a cup of bourbon, and some maple syrup! Egads, man; either this gal doesn't like the taste of bear meat, or she prefers to drink her wild cuisine. Busy recipes like this only serve to perpetuate the erroneous popular notion that bear meat is strong or unpalatable.

It is not. Our family has so far eaten three different bears. Bear roasts cooked just like any domestic beef roast are tender and tasty.

Far too many wild-game recipes rely on the two major culprits in the great cover-up: cream of mushroom soup and dry onion soup mix. I understand the temptation. The stuff is tasty, and you can cover a multitude of cooking sins with this sodium-charged combo. A Great Plains buffalo chip or an old Alton Bog beaver slow-cooked in a Crock-Pot with the soup-onion combo would probably keep a group of hungry hunters coming back for more. (Diane claims that the sodium hit in the soup mix is worse for me than the buffalo chip.)

Again, we have found that when it comes to wild-game cooking, simplicity is the key. National wild-cooking writer John Cartier writes: "Don't get taken in with what I call 'Fantasy Cooking.' That's the supposedly gourmet meal preparation you see on TV and in cooking magazines. I usually don't use recipes that call for more than six ingredients because I want to highlight the unique flavor of wild food, not destroy it with ordinary stuff you can buy in markets."

Cartier also notes that "the notion still persists that game cookery involves sorcery and mysterious processes to get the 'wild taste' out. The misconceptions about gamey flavors are slowly but surely being dispelled . . ."

37

Of Heaths and Hummocks

From all reports, the legendary Maine Guide, like so many of our institutions, is undergoing profound change. The Maine Guide of yore was simply a woods-savvy individual who had hunted and fished enough to know how to show others the way for a few dollars a day. The early Maine Guides never took a test. Most of them got their licenses after a Maine game warden decided, from a short chat, that an applicant was fit to be a Maine Guide. Today, more and more of our Registered Maine Guides get their guide's license by taking formal instruction and then passing a series of written and oral tests administered by the Maine Department of Inland Fisheries and Wildlife.

Now this is not altogether bad, and is certainly in keeping with the times. Veteran guides have been known to scoff while making the observation that many of these new "school-taught" guides just wanted to get a guide's patch for their wool jackets

Photo by V. Paul Reynolds

Is this a bog, a swamp, or a swale? It depends. You'll have to consult with a Registered Maine Guide to get an authoritative answer.

and have no plans to guide for a living. So? It does take some smarts and commitment to pass the test, and anyone who makes the grade has a reason to be proud of his or her accomplishment.

It does strike me, though, that there is a conspicuous and glaring gap in the curriculum of most of the new training programs for aspiring Maine Guides. These new Maine Guides, especially those who grew up in Newark or White Plains, all mispronounce a critical word used by all Maine Guides. The word is *heath*. Regardless of what Webster's may say, all Maine woodsmen and seasoned Maine Guides pronounce this word "hayth," not "heeth," as far too many newly licensed Maine Guides seem to be doing.

If you are a newly licensed Maine Guide, you would be advised to practice the proper Maine pronunciation of this word until it becomes a natural part of your guide lexicon. Say again, "Joe, you work your way slowly around the south side of that 'hayth,' and I'll meet you at about noon on the north end of the hummock."

Speaking of a Maine Guide's lexicon, any guide worth his salt will not only use the Maine pronunciation, but will also know the subtle distinctions in the definitions of unique geological locales. Here are some must-know woods places that all Maine Guides should be familiar with:

Swale: A swale is a slight depression that runs along the contour of the land. That is to say, it is level all along its length. It can be deep or shallow, or even hidden (a ditch filled with gravel and capped with topsoil), and the dirt from digging the swale is usually used to make a berm on the downhill side. A common-size swale is two or three feet wide. Of course, you can make them any size you want. An important distinction is that a swale is not a drain; it's a water-collection device. The cheapest way to store water is in the soil. And of course, by stopping the runoff, it prevents erosion as well.

Heath: A heath or heathland is a dwarf-shrub habitat found on mainly infertile acidic soils, characterized by open, low-growing woody vegetation, often dominated by plants of the Ericaceae family. It is similar to moorland, but is generally warmer and drier.

Bog: So what the heck is a bog anyway? Is it a lake? A swamp? A marsh? A farm? Or just a funny-sounding word we made up? Actually, a bog is an area of soft, marshy ground, usually located near wetlands, where cranberries love to grow. During the harvest, water is pumped in and out so it gets really wet. Which explains why we like to wear waders. It's also what makes the cranberry such a unique fruit.

Logan: A swamp or a bog.

Hummock: A knoll or tract of land higher than a surrounding marshy area.

Of course, these are just the rudimentary usages that newly licensed guides should master. Most truly dedicated and conscientious Maine Guides never stop expanding their lexicon when it comes to naming and describing the infinite and disparate topography that comprises the fabled Maine North Woods.

To this end, accomplished Maine Guide Randy Spencer has made a valuable contribution in a chapter on this subject in his delightful book, *Where Cool Waters Flow*. Here are some that are guaranteed to salt the vocabulary of the most experienced and venerated Registered Maine Guides.

Swallett: A place in the woods where a small, gurgling brook suddenly disappears and runs underground.

Chiminage: A fee charged for using the Maine woods.

Gnarr: A bulbous, sinewy area on a tree.

Zuckle: A stump that is cut close to the ground.

Grike: An opening in a fence that will allow a person (but not an animal) to get through.

Eyot: Pronounced "ite," this is a small island located in a river or lake.

38

The Cookie Eater

There is an avid deer hunter from Hampden who is doing his fair share to help improve the survival odds for Maine whitetails. He has taken up bow hunting.

A gun hunter for most of his life, this Hampden man decided that hunting deer with a bow might provide more of a challenge. The idea began to hold some appeal when *Northwoods Sporting Journal's* bow writer Josh Cottrell told him that, indeed, bow hunting a deer is ground zero when it comes to hunting methods. "There's nothing quite like it," said Cottrell. "Not only is it more challenging than a gun hunt, because you must get close to your prey, but it's also truly the primal hunt, up close and personal."

After purchasing a high-tech compound bow and practicing all summer from a tree stand on a backyard target, the Hampden man accepted an invitation to bow-hunt deer in Carroll

County, Maryland, which is America's deer central. For five days the Hampden hunter sat in a tree stand way up in a hickory tree, within eyeshot of a field of soybeans. He said that he had never seen anything quite like it in the deer woods.

"There were deer everywhere," he exclaimed. "Trouble is, most of the deer I saw were either on my way *to* the stand in the morning or on my way *out* of the stand after sundown." He said that on two separate occasions he jumped deer right out of the middle of a soybean field. "I couldn't believe it," he said. "These deer were bedded down midday, right out in the middle of these soybeans! It was like flushing partridge out of a brush pile."

He said that in four days he logged about thirty hours sitting in the hickory tree and experienced just two deer encounters. "I had a small buck come to my bleat call, and he hung around a while but never came close enough for a shot," he recalled. "In the other heart-pumper, a small doe looked up at me just as I started to draw back the bowstring. Yep, I got busted," he said.

The Hampden man said that being a Maine hunter, he was used to putting in long hours in a tree stand without seeing any deer. "The weather is milder during the bow season, which is nothing like trying to ward off a November chill. Late September in Maryland is really nice," he says. "Songbirds flit about. Fat gray squirrels root around for nuts and scold you for being in their tree. Turkey vultures hover above the canopy as though waiting for a new gut pile. The times goes by. You read some, and eat a lot of cookies."

The Hampden hunter, who wishes to remain anonymous, said that he returned from Maryland without releasing an arrow. A few days after his return, he decided to take advantage of his bonus doe permit and give Maine a try. He erected his tree stand in a deer swamp he was familiar with in the Thomaston area.

Photo by Scott Reynolds

This is me, the Cookie Eater, humping a pack in the Colorado mountains. I took up bow hunting late in my hunting career and got hopelessly hooked. It is the ultimate challenge for a hunter who gets satisfaction from trying to outwit his quarry on more even ground.

He said that ironically, during his two-day hunt back in Maine, he came really close to finally releasing an arrow at a deer. "I had been sitting in this tree about four hours. I had eaten, oh, I don't know, maybe five or six cookies. The sun was down. It was very quiet. Nothing stirred. Good time for a bleat call, I thought," he recalled. "Unknown to me, while I was rummaging around in my daypack for the bleat call, a doe was coming my way along the game trail that I was overlooking. You guessed it. Not twenty yards from me, she either heard me or saw me move. She bounded into the brush. A few snorts and she was long gone," he said.

The following day the hapless Hampden bow hunter was walking down an access road at a state park. Dressed in full camo and toting a bow equipped with a quiver of arrows, he walked by an elderly couple strolling hand in hand. Obviously, leaf-peepers getting some fresh air. He said that they looked startled.

"Good morning," he greeted the strollers.

"Oh, is it bow season now?" the man asked.

"Yes," the hunter replied, smiling.

"Then we better get out of here," the stroller said, taking his wife by the elbow and starting to turn back.

"Oh, don't do that," the hunter said. "Nothing to be concerned about; it's very safe. I mostly just sit up in a tree all day and eat cookies."

39

Last-Ditch Pot Roast

It wasn't like the hunter hadn't gone a season without tagging a deer before. He was proud of his average—a deer about every other year throughout his deer-hunting career. Still, this would be his second year with an empty freezer, even though he had hunted diligently through the bow season, the November firearms season, and nearly two weeks of black-powder hunting.

It was the last day of the two-week-long black-powder season. The day before, with a tracking snow, he had jumped nine deer all bedded down in a fir thicket. Hoping to fill his bonus doe permit, he had deliberately picked a medium-size track and stayed on it all day. The deer knew there was a predator back there, and took the hunter through the usual alder tangles and mucky hellholes, trying to discourage its pursuer. By day's end, the deer still hadn't shown itself. Just before giving up the quest, the wet and tired hunter noticed a newcomer's track. A coyote!

"Damn," he said to himself. "Now I'm competing with coyotes." The coyote was on the deer's track and, apparently, closer
to the quarry than he. *Time to call it a day,* he thought, and
began backtracking his way back to the truck.

As it had for so many other fall mornings, the alarm awak-
ened the hunter at four a.m. He was tempted to roll over and
declare the hunting season over, but there was still a tracking
snow, and it tugged at him. It was the last day, and he knew from
experience that it pays to persevere if you want to hang a deer.

Back in the same woods, he found lots of tracks. Too many.
It was confusing. He decided to still-hunt around the fir thickets on the chance that he might get lucky. By three in the afternoon, a chill took him and he decided to accept the inevitable:
"It's over for this year. Time to go home and get warm. It's been
fun all the same. Maybe next year," he consoled himself.

Then he saw it. On the edge of the thicket there was a deer
carcass—a fresh kill. It was a medium-size doe, obviously taken
down and eaten alive by coyotes. There were signs of a struggle,
the entrails spread around with a lot of hair, and one of the
hindquarters chewed up pretty good.

For a moment, the hunter studied the death scene with
curiosity. From the tracks it looked like a pair of coyotes had
killed the young doe. *What a way to go,* he thought.

He started to walk away, but had second thoughts. There
was the smell of viscera in the cold air, but he turned the deer
over just the same and saw that the other hindquarter was
untouched by the previous diners. Taking out his knife, he
skinned back the hide and cut off a large chunk of the hindquarter. Once the meat was separated, he stepped away and gave it
the sniff test. "Hmmm, this is okay. It'll do as a roast," he told
himself. He placed the meat in a big Ziploc bag he carried and
put it in his hunting daypack.

Back at the truck, while removing the 209 primer from his muzzleloader, he got to thinking. "Maybe I've discovered a new way to hunt in Maine's coyote-rich environment. Just get on a coyote track and let it take you to its next kill. You don't even need to carry a gun. Just a knife."

The next day, the hunter cleaned up the chunk of coyote kill and wrapped it with butcher's twine into a two-pound pot roast. He rolled it in flour with salt and pepper and seared it in a hot frying pan. Then he placed it in his wife's new Hamilton Beach Crock-Pot with some peeled potatoes, onions, and carrots. To the Crock-Pot he added two cloves of garlic, a can of Swanson's low-sodium beef broth, a cup of orange juice, a cup of red wine, and a dash of Worcestershire sauce. He then deglazed the frying pan with some hot water and poured the drippings over the roast. He put the Crock-Pot on the low setting and let it cook, covered, for about eight hours.

While his wife was away, he set up a card table in the living room near the TV with place settings for two. He included a candle and some wineglasses. Upon his wife's return, he invited her to dine with him at his impromptu dinner theater. They turned on an old movie and the hunter served his wife a dish he called "Last-Ditch Pot Roast." She said that it was by far the best pot roast she had ever eaten!

The hunter and his wife raised their glasses and toasted the end of another Maine deer season.

40

Tree Stands for Seniors

If hunting from tree stands is a new experience for you, or if you are an experienced tree-stand hunter who has been operating under the misconception that tree stands are not potentially hazardous to your health, do a quick Google search on the Internet of "tree-stand safety." The glare from the amber light of warnings about the safe use of tree stands should give you second thoughts.

The record is clear: Every hunting season, hunters, in an effort to elevate themselves and their scents above the ground and the game, fall out of trees. Some receive disabling back and neck injuries. Some are even killed in their falls from tree stands, no matter how well designed or rigged.

I have been messing around with tree stands for years. A number of homebuilt wooden ladder stands have been assembled in my workshop. I also own a couple of manufactured portable

Photo by Diane Reynolds

Seniors Pete Caron (left) and the author practice with their climbing stands before the big hunt.

seat stands that I have used for hunting deer and bear. With fingers crossed, I can boast that I have never even had a close call in a tree stand—at least not until this September.

In need of a so-called climbing tree stand for a bear hunt, I borrowed a "climber" from my son Josh. Over the phone he gave me verbal instructions. Wanting to get the hang of it before actually hunting, I practiced climbing a birch tree in the backyard. I made two mistakes at the outset. First, I used a smooth-barked tree, and, second, I did not secure the platform section of the climber to the upper seat climbing section. You guessed it. On my first ascent, at an elevation of approximately twelve feet, the lower platform fell away from my feet and slid down the tree to the ground. I was left dangling, swinging in the wind, held up only by my elbows on the seat section of the climber. In an attempt not to sound panicky, I called in my most-controlled baritone to Diane, who was working in her flower garden on the other side of the house. "Say, hon, could you come here for a second?"

No answer. My elbows were tiring fast.

I screamed in high-pitched, full-blown panic: "Diane, Diane! Come quick!"

We learned later, after I'd managed to make a shin-burning, controlled-crash slide down the tree, that she had been talking on her cell phone and never heard my cries for help.

Frankly, that was a sphincter-tightening experience. I've slid down trees before, no sweat, and I'm a pretty agile guy for my years, but I'm no gymnast. You try making the awkward conversion from your elbow perch on the climber rails to the tree trunk.

Anyway, I'll have no part of tree stands that are designed to be "climbers." They are death traps designed by youthful sadists intent on scaring old hunters half to death. I'm sticking with the more-traditional portable-seat stands that include a portable climbing ladder attached to the tree.

My bear-hunting buddy Ron—a robust man in the 200-pound range who is longer in the tooth than even I—refuses ever to elevate himself in the woods after having fallen off a ladder stand from twelve feet or so. He hunts bear and deer from ground blinds. Being at ground level at a distance of thirty feet from an active bear bait doesn't seem to give him pause. "I'd rather have a bear breathing down my neck than a doctor at the emergency room," he says. He was soon to learn that you are only as safe as you think you are.

Let me set the stage: Ron's ground blind is a scant piece of flat ground that looks down a very steep bank. At the bottom of the steep grade, the terrain flattens out. There he has his bait site. It is, as bear bait sites go, an ideal setup. The bears hang out close by in the cool bog not far from the site. Ron has killed a couple of big bears there. Diane also got her first bear there, as did two retired game-warden acquaintances of ours. The hunter sits in the blind next to the hill on an old metal folding chair. Getting the bear carcass up the hill is a challenge, even with an ATV and strong ropes.

This September, on his first afternoon in the ground blind, after one of Diane's sumptuous bear-camp meals and a generous piece of blackberry pie, Ron apparently dozed off during his bear-bait vigil. As he later recounted for us back at camp (when we inquired about the cut on his nose and neck), Ron decided to make an involuntary, unscheduled visitation of the bait site at about five p.m. Not a good time to be at the bait. He got there by leaning back and falling out of his chair and rolling down the hill with his .308 Savage held above his head like Lee Marvin in *Sands of Iwo Jima*. Not seriously injured, luckily, he compounded his lack-of-stealth faux pas by checking the safety on his gun. Apparently damaged in the fall, it was not working. The .308 promptly discharged.

An intrepid hunter who never quits, Ron, ignoring his facial cuts, clambered back up the hill, tidied up his ground blind, and renewed his bear vigil. He said that it was easier staying awake after that.

For some reason, the bear never showed.

Part IV:

Memories

41

Victor's Forever Day

On the heels of a windy, rainy night, the October morning broke clear over the bay. Shafts of sunlight found their way through the last lingering cloud bank on the horizon. In the marsh grass along the estuary, Canada geese could be heard but not seen. The day held great promise.

As we gathered up our setters and shotguns for the day's hunt, Victor paused to savor the scene. Gesturing with his cup of coffee, he commented, "What a beautiful spot. I'm gonna come back in two weeks and hunt here with my son."

For a while that morning, Victor's hunt was textbook upland hunting. His friend and hunting companion's English setter Max performed with pluck and precision. Victor took down two birds. One of his kills was a splendid cock pheasant that would have gotten away had it not been for Victor's skill with a shotgun.

Courtesy of V. Paul Reynolds

Victor Schibelli

As the dog ranged out in search of new scent, the men talked. Victor—a retired game warden whose rugged Italian good looks belied his seventy-two years—enjoyed sharing warden stories with his companions. Again, he spoke of his son and reaffirmed his plan to "return soon to hunt with young Victor." And then, without warning, Victor collapsed. On that perfect October morning, strolling through knee-deep clover under cloudless blue skies, when all seemed right with the world, Victor died. Although his hunting companion tried for a half-hour to revive Victor, his desperate efforts were in vain. At the hospital, doctors said that Victor was dead when he hit the ground from a "massive coronary."

All friends are special, and so was Victor. When you share hunting camps and fishing trips with outdoor people, you get to know them. Victor was a gentle, easygoing person who loved his God, his wife, his family and friends, and his outdoor world. The son of Italian immigrants, Victor often said unabashedly, "I love my country." He knew his wild mushrooms, and his way around an Italian kitchen. Once, while he and I were rustling up some bacon and eggs outside a tent site in an early-morning drizzle, I overheard him singing like Tony Bennett. I could never get him to do it again, even after two glasses of his home-made wine that he had dubbed "the Recipe."

Victor was a kindred spirit who will be missed, and his memory has left an imprint that will not easily fade for the rest of us who shared his outdoor world. At first, it seemed wrong that death should take our friend on such a perfect October day. But, looking back, it's beginning to make sense. Victor was a contented man with few regrets and very much at peace with himself and his Creator.

Shortly after Victor's death, while editing a column for the *Northwoods Sporting Journal*, some words from outdoor columnist Patricia Robbins got me thinking again about our friend, the late Victor Schibelli:

> If it were a choice when we leave this world for another, I would ask for autumn days that stretched before me like summer vacations when I was a child. I would want to see the sun rise and draw the dew from the grass. To have the evening air bring my breath to sight.
>
> I would ask for trees so beautiful they would take my breath away. To see all of wildlife at its prime. Fur full, feathers fluffed. I would want peace of mind. To dance with the leaves as they swirl about forever graceful, across the mountains and the meadows, then quietly come to rest against the walls of stone. To feel the wind upon my face, forever cool, forever fall.

42

Some Special Moments

The heavens declare the glory of God; and the firmament shows His handiwork.
—*Psalm 19*

Maine's legendary outdoor columnist, the late Bud Leavitt, once counseled me when I was a young newspaperman at the *Bangor Daily News* about the importance of building a storehouse of fond memories. Bud knew that I was close with the dollar and more prone to spend a little extra on tangibles—a new gun or fly rod—than on a vacation away for me and my wife. He got me thinking about the true worth of memory building. Over time, Bud's advice has proven wise and worthy.

Come to think of it, collecting good memories that spring from special moments is what energizes most outdoor people that I have known—Bud included. Memories, like an old friend,

Photo by V. Paul Reynolds

This is dockside on an early June morning at Grants Camps at Kennebago Lake. Casting a fly line for surfacing trout from one of these fabled Rangeley boats is a special moment.

can be called upon in time of need. This month, for reasons that I don't fully understand, fishing fever has a grip on my psyche with a preoccupation that is unfamiliar to me. In past years, I have always patiently avoided fishing during the limbo month in Maine we call April.

Today is the first day of open-water fishing in Maine. The stream behind the house is still locked in ice. I just cleared my driveway of wet, heavy snow, and more is in the forecast. Above the snow depth behind the house, only a plastic antler can be seen of the full-size decoy deer that I use for bow practice. The thermometer has stubbornly hovered near the 30-degree mark.

These are the times to call on those priceless memories, to dip into the storage bin of special outdoor moments.

I was a Yankee flatlander in a flat-bottom rowboat alone on a trout pond in Colorado's Flat Tops Wilderness area. On the southwest side of the pond, craggy cliffs and scattered softwoods spiraled a thousand feet above the high-elevation pond, which was at 11,500 feet above sea level. On the other side, just above the tree line, open meadows ascended upward. Amid the wind-blown green sweetgrass, bright blue wildflowers shimmered like sunlit sequins in a verdant sea.

Soon the fish began to surface-feed. Small cutthroats and Eastern brookies were slurping a hatch that I didn't recognize. No matter; a #16 Adams was doing the trick nicely. I caught a couple of brookies for supper, and released a handful of pan-size fish. Defying the best advice of veteran Western anglers, I attached a Hornberg to my 4X tippet. On the second cast, a slashing rise surprised me and a two-pound cutthroat struggled for freedom. At that very moment, other things happened. A bull elk began bugling from the craggy terrain above. And, almost on cue, like divine choreography, the black clouds on the western horizon shifted and shafts of sunlight angled through the upper canyon and illuminated the pond.

Talk about a quality wilderness experience! The scene over-whelmed me with a totality I'd never experienced before in the outdoors. So taken was I by it all that the handsome trout on the end of my fly line became secondary to the natural panorama unfolding there in the solitude of the Colorado Rockies. Mes-merized by the magnitude of the scenic splendor, I just sat there, slack-jawed. Fishing had taken a backseat. I cannot to this day honestly remember whether I boated that trout or it simply took advantage of my unattended fly line and slipped away. It really didn't matter. And I am a serious, overly prideful angler.

Another time, while camping in northern Maine, I decided on impulse to hike into a remote trout pond in the pouring rain. The forecast was not hopeful, and it was out of character for me to walk three miles in a downpour to fish for trout, especially at midday. As I stood beneath an overhanging hemlock bough beside the pond at high noon, the rain stopped as if on cue. The pond became a mirror and the mist began to rise. Across the pond, near an inlet, the pond's mirror-like sheen was broken by the telltale dimple of an occasional feeding trout.

Silently, I assembled my fly rod, attached a #12 grasshopper, and slid the outfitter's canoe into the water. The rain held off, and as I glided the canoe toward the inlet and the unsuspecting trout, I breathed in deeply, savoring the moment. Through the mist, I unfurled my fly line and placed the artificial terrestrial on the assorted targets.

Trout, big, beautifully colored brookies, came to my presentation as if bent on suicide. It was a grasshopper day! You wanted to freeze time forever. Then it was over. The pond became still, the dimples ceased, and soon it started to rain again.

Like my memory of fishing in the Rockies, that day in the rain was a special moment. Thinking back, what I still cherish—along with the memorable fishing—is the remarkable, if not uncanny, timing of it all, and the sweet and pungent smell of the rain-soaked North Woods, the fragrance after the rain.

Memories. Special moments that endure and are always there when you need them.

43

Slouch of Slough Creek

Greg Jalbert grew up fly-fishing the Allagash with his grandfather. Today, Jalbert field-tests fishing gear for L.L. Bean's fly-fishing journal.

Jalbert recounts a field exercise testing gear on the Wind River out West. His recollections of leaping rainbows and shadows creeping up canyon walls is poetry—up to a point.

Having fished Montana and Wyoming on a dream trip last summer with my wife, I enjoyed reading aloud Jalbert's account of his trip to Diane the other day as she drove us south on I-95. Golly, we did what he did! Not only did he discover the wonders of the #14 Parachute Adams, but Jalbert also got off the beaten path and pursued fourteen-inch brookies in feeder streams when he could have nymphed for trophy rainbows. That's precisely what we did near Brooks Lake in Wyoming.

Of course, Jalbert had a different arrangement than Diane and I: The folks at Bean's paid Mr. Jalbert to fish the Wind River; Diane and I paid Bean's.

A fashion-conscious angler I have never been. But after saving and planning for our Western dream trip, we wanted things "to be right." We sought advice from Bean's. As always, they were helpful. Diane and I got outfitted to the hilt. I came away with a new fishing vest, a pack frame, a float tube, a special hat, new neoprene waders, and color-coordinated wading shoes. We were equipped.

After a long drive cross-country, we set up camp at Slough Creek in Montana near our new Maine friends, Gifford and Annabelle. They—veteran Slough Creek visitors—had encouraged us to come West. In our planning sessions, we had nailed down travel routes, camping gear, and park rules, but had never discussed fishing attire.

"So here's the plan," Gifford said, as we made plans around the campfire for the first day of fishing. "Meet at the trailhead at six a.m. sharp. Then we hike the four miles to Second Meadow. Cutthroats the size of footballs. Pack a lunch."

That night we packed, almost ceremoniously. With great care, L.L. Bean neoprene waders, studded Aqua Stealth wading shoes, Magalloway vest, and all the rest were tucked into my backpack. Total estimated gross weight: twenty-five to thirty pounds.

As the Montana dawn sent shafts of light through the lodgepole pines above our camp, Diane and I exited our tent camper feeling prepared and eager for our first day on the creek. Backpacks on and rod tubes in hand, we greeted our "guide," Gifford.

Pleasantries were exchanged and we began the long ascent to Second Meadow. As Gifford led the way, Diane and I exchanged glances. It was noticeable that this experienced Fisher of the West had not been exposed to L.L. Bean. Our pathfinder

Gifford Stevens fishing the Magalloway River.

gave new meaning to simplicity: no backpack stuffed with
waders and shoes, no rod tube, no Polartec warm-up jacket. A
T-shirt, a pair of faded wind pants, and an old, stained, wide-
brimmed hat covered this man. On his feet there were no Gore-
Tex Knife Edge trail boots. He wore sandals and carried his fly
rod in two pieces. His extra equipment consisted of two water
bottles, and a small fanny pack served as his fishing vest.

From our friend Gifford, we learned much that wonderful
July day in Montana. He was a picture not only of simplicity,
but of an angler out of himself and given to total concentration.
For him, the focus was on the fishing, not on what he wore or
carried. He braved the cold water and waded to the best pools in
his wind pants and sandals. The high Montana sun dried him.
The tattered, wide-brimmed hat kept his head cool. His lunch
was a bag of trail mix.

The time that he would have used getting in and out of waders, wading shoes, and vest was devoted to his obsession: getting the fly on the water, and getting the drift just right. He fished with a vengeance. And he was good with a fly rod, very good. The cutthroats were footballs, and Gifford outfished us three to one.

Back to Mr. Jalbert, the man who has the L.L Bean job that so many of us would like to have. Jalbert's theme seems to be that technology can make the angler. He writes: "Technology had finally brought solace to this obsession." This closing sentence is then followed by a long list of "field-proven gear" used by Jalbert on the Wind River. Of course, he is paid to say that, and he has come a long way since those days when he fished in leaky old waders on the Allagash, or struggled with cheap fly rods that didn't cast very well.

Perhaps he has a point. There's nothing like a well-crafted fly rod and the sound of a quality reel. But fly fishing's attraction for me has always been its simplicity. It was good to be brought back, to be reminded of this by my friend Gifford, the Slouch of Slough Creek.

44

First Fiddleheads

For those of us in more northerly Maine, there is at long last a
hint of spring in the air. Soon it will be time to go fiddleheadin'.

For the True Gatherer, the first fiddlehead green that pokes
through the sandy silt in the lowlands near brooks and streams
stirs an inner joy. I count myself among the True Gatherers:
Finding wild things to eat that have not been plastic-wrapped
by industrialized man is a source of intense satisfaction and
accomplishment.

In fact, the need to gather for nourishment—whether by
planting and growing, picking, killing, or catching—seems to
be instinctive. Where does it come from, this atavistic yearning?
Who knows. But it's there for those of us who must go out and
find wild mushrooms, grow potatoes in rich dirt, or kill a
majestic wild animal for its meat.

Photo by V. Paul Reynolds

A *bowl of fresh-picked ostrich ferns.*

For some, spring is just a distant promise until the first robin is sighted, or the evening song of the amphibians is heard at sunset. Diane and I find spring in the first feed of fiddleheads. Out back of our place, the stream has rid itself of an ice-encrusted shoreline and the runoff has started to subside.

Our fiddlehead vigil has begun. From the field, I can see the sandy bar on the other side of the stream where it makes a bend. As the days warm, I will remain watchful, making a daily check for "conditions."

With fiddleheads, timing is everything.

Once, while on a trout-fishing trip in northern Aroostook County, Diane and I by sheer good luck brought home a memory unmatched in our Gatherers' Chronicle. On our third day of tenting and fishing, unusually warm weather for late May was forcing us to break camp early. We were out of ice and our remaining food was about to spoil. That morning, while working our way down a brook to a remote trout pond, we came upon a patch of fiddleheads. While picking some of these tasty greens for supper, we discovered some glacial ledges near the stream that still held winter ice. Long story short: Our trip back was a True Gatherer's dream. My pack basket contained freshly picked fiddleheads and four nice brookies, all cooled down by large chunks of blue ice. No charge for the ice, either.

The stream out back is a long way from Aroostook County's trout country, and Diane and I are not alone. Here, there are other True Gatherers also keeping an eye on "our" fiddlehead grounds.

There is intense competition for nature's offerings, so late pickers may wind up scrounging for remnants. We must remain alert.

Soon the dry tangled lowlands near the stream will take on splotches of green. Some warm, rainy days will precede the debut of the skunk cabbage. Not long after, usually following a couple of wonderful, warm spring afternoons, the first nubs of the ostrich fern (fiddleheads) will make themselves barely visible beneath the dark, beet-colored root clumps.

With a bucket in one hand and a walking stick for stability, we will forge the fast-moving stream in our waders. Then, among the skunk cabbages and the first hatch of bugs, we will bend down and snap off these green, curled ferns one by one. Clutching our pickings as if they were panned gold, we'll head back across the stream and straight for the kitchen. After a careful cleaning, the fiddleheads will be steamed, perhaps with a piece of bacon.

Then they will be served. Maine fiddlehead greens as fresh as they can ever be. Drum roll, please. Spring is now. As we savor the unique flavor, as well as the seasonal rite for its own sake, we will know for sure that we have outlasted another long Maine winter, and that the best gathering of the year is yet to come.

45

Bringing Her Along

In Maine, as in the rest of the country, more and more women are getting serious about the great outdoors and becoming outdoorswomen. This is for the most part a good thing, an inevitable offshoot of our cultural revolution and the modern woman's quest for personal independence. Historically, Maine had its own Annie Oakleys long before women were fighting for the right to vote. In the days before suffrage, there weren't many Maine women who could "rope, ride, and shoot"—or cast a long fly line—but the ones who could were good at it, and are part of Maine's outdoor folklore.

Fast forward.

Today, there is a formal program for those women who want to learn to hunt and fish: BOW (Becoming an Outdoors-Woman).

This is a wonderful program offered and sanctioned by the Maine Department of Inland Fisheries and Wildlife. Thanks to BOW, dozens of women have been able to acquire outdoor knowledge and skills from patient professionals rather than from a significant intimate whose strong suit might not be sharing his outdoors savvy with the woman of his dreams.

Maine has a term for this outdoor-learning process. It's called "bringing somebody along." From the time I was old enough to walk in the woods, I was "brought along" by my dad, as is the case with my sons and so many other Maine outdoorsmen. The classroom was always there wherever we hunted, fished, or camped. And we learned—not only how to catch and clean a fish, or to hunt and care for wild meat—but literally hundreds of other less-obvious or mundane outdoor skills that became second nature. For example, how to find dry firewood in the driving rain, how a choke works on an outboard motor, or how to flare a copper pipe for a gaslight hookup.

Diane, my wife, grew up with an outdoorsman father. While she had great times at camp, and learned to drive her dad's old army jeep on back roads, she was never "brought along" in the ways of the outdoors. Later in life, with children grown and a teaching career behind her, my lifelong passion for hunting and fishing beckoned her. She enrolled in a number of BOW program offerings, and came away with good basic knowledge of fly fishing, outdoor cooking, canoeing, gun safety, and marksmanship. In ten years, she has learned a lot by doing. It has been a bittersweet experience to watch her surpass me as a fly fisher and a marksman, but I have learned to adjust.

Last week, though, she and I came face-to-face with a gaping void in her repertoire of outdoor skills. A thorough woman who is intense about always being prepared, she asked me for some basic instruction before striking out on an all-women trip to Montana with my sister in our pickup and tent camper.

"Gee, Diane," I said, rolling my eyes, "it's not exactly rocket science. Just follow the signs to Bozeman. What do you want to know?"

"Well, you know, hon," she said, "I ought to know how to do the stuff you normally do, like how to change a tire on the truck, how to put up the camper, turn on the propane—that sort of stuff."

We went at it, and did she ever get checked out. What I thought would be a half-hour briefing turned into a protracted three-day tutorial on tires, tire pressures, tire gauges, socket wrenches, fuse boxes, fuse replacement, trailer hitches, ball sizes,

Photo by V. Paul Reynolds

Diane Reynolds with her first wild turkey. Since then she has brought home deer, bear, moose, elk and a few grouse.

tongue weights, propane tanks, two-stage regulators, left-hand threads, 12-volt deep-cycle Marine batteries, AC-DC conversion, properties of graphite as a dry lubricant, and so forth.

She seemed pleased and confident when her instruction was concluded.

"Good," she said. "I think I'm ready."

"It would have been easier to prepare you for a moon shot," I said.

As it turned out, much of what Diane didn't know were things that most experienced, "brought-along" outdoorsmen just soak up along the way. While Diane learned a lot at her three different BOW sessions, she missed out on some basics, as enumerated above.

The BOW planners deserve a lot of credit just the same. They have worked diligently at providing students with a well-rounded curriculum. They even have a program called "Beyond BOW," which is a kind of advanced-degree program. Still, nothing is being offered on socket wrenches and left-hand threads.

At no small risk, might I propose a new course offering for perhaps the basic BOW program that encompasses so many of these not-so-obvious, mundane skills that an accomplished outdoorswoman must master if she is going to become truly capable and independent in the outdoors. This course, however compressed, would be kind of a preparatory schooling for those aspiring outdoorswomen who were never "brought along," so to speak.

By the way, my wife the outdoorswoman reported in by cell phone last night. She was passing through the South Dakota Badlands. Rapid City was just ahead. The rig was humming nicely. She said there had been no need to rely on any of her newly acquired skills, but that it "felt good to be ready, just in case."

46

Dog-Days Trout

Back along, a column I wrote about Maine's specially designated "remote trout ponds" spurred quite a bit of reader interest. An offer to e-mail a list of these 176 remote ponds to anyone requesting it brought dozens and dozens of requests. They are still coming in.

Enter Joe Pratt. A capable, meticulous fly fisherman who works as a financial planner in the Bangor area, Joe is one of those successful young professionals who, in my opinion, works too much and fishes too little. I know because I once walked that trail. When I talked with Joe last week, he said that he hadn't wetted a fly this season. "Not good, Joe," I reproached, shaking my head, "Life's too short."

As we talked, I recalled in my mind the June night a few years back when Joe and my son Scotty were overtaken by darkness at one of these remote ponds. Neither man had a flashlight.

Photo by V. Paul Reynolds

Mainers Scott Reynolds (left) and Fred Hurley prepare to launch their float tubes for some early morning fly-fishing on a remote trout pond in the Northwoods.

Hiking out on a rough trail in the pitch black was out of the question, so they hunkered down till dawn's early light. Meanwhile, anxious wives notified the Maine Warden Service. When these two "lost souls" walked out of the woods just after daybreak the next day, District Warden Andy Glidden was at the trailhead to greet them and about to start a search. Assorted admonishments followed from loved ones about the Boy Scout motto, etc. Warden Glidden, to his credit, reportedly offered no lectures to the "missing" anglers. What Warden Glidden probably didn't know is that both fishermen were trained in outdoor survival by the US Air Force.

Joe told me that although he hadn't fished this season, he had been thinking trout. In fact, he had read my column, gotten the list of Maine's 176 remote trout ponds, and was inspired— not only to go fishing, but to do some further research on these remote ponds, organize his data, and run it through some spreadsheet software in his computer. What he has done is prepare an alphabetical listing of the ponds, along with the following information: pond acreage, location, county, appropriate page in the DeLorme Gazetteer, and pond altitude.

Obviously, this adds immeasurably to the convenience factor for folks who share my goal in life: to fish all 176 of these ponds. Of particular interest to me is the listing of pond altitudes. A few of these remote ponds are at altitudes in excess of 2,000 feet above sea level. In fact, one pond in Oxford County is at 3,425 feet. Why is altitude of interest? Well, as Joe notes, altitude affects air temperature, which in turn affects water temperature, insect hatches, and fish-activity levels.

Bottom line: Die-hard trout anglers discouraged by warming waters and lethargic trout during the Dog Days of August might want to check out some of these higher-altitude remote ponds. From Joe's list, here are fifteen of the highest-altitude remote ponds in Maine:

Aziscohos Pond, 2,100; Cape Horn Pond, 1,900; Clearwater Pond, 1,960; Clish Pond, 1,820; Eddy Pond, 2,625; Helen Pond, 2,050; High Pond, 2,080; Ledge Pond, 2,987; Little Swift Pond, 2,450; Midway Pond, 2,725; Moxie Pond, 2,375; Northwest Pond, 2,090; Saddleback Pond, 2,100; Speck Pond, 3,425, and Tumbledown Pond, 2,660.

The highest-altitude pond, Speck, is a small, nine-acre pond in Grafton Township in Oxford County. Of the 176 designated remote trout ponds, 89 of them are located in Piscataquis County. Please note that vehicular access of any kind (this includes ATVs) is prohibited into these ponds.

Our thanks to Joe Pratt for sharing the list. May he find more time to wet a fly in the days and years ahead, and may he always bring his flashlight. (A complete version of the Pratt List is found in Chapter 55.)

47

Wild Berry Fever

I saw the bearded old man coming toward me through the jack firs. A short distance from my tree stand, he paused, looked up, and breathed hard in the cold November morning. There was a scowl on his face and in his voice.

"What are you doing in my tree?" he asked.

"I'm hunting deer," I answered. After explaining that I thought the tree was on my small woodlot behind my newly purchased home, he set me straight. As it turned out, he was right. I had misread my new property lines and erected my portable tree stand where I was not wanted. Over the years, my sporadic attempts to win over the old man and secure permission to hunt his land were unsuccessful. In 1996, I shot a fine eight-point buck that ran from my property onto the old man's. I trespassed to retrieve my buck.

Photo by Diane Reynolds

For the True Gatherer, foraging for wild berries on a sunny day when there is an afternoon breeze stirring is a special kind of peace.

From our short talks, I learned that the old man had retired from factory work in Fall River, Massachusetts. During the war he had served on a submarine and recalled shooting a deck-mounted machine gun at Japanese Zeros. He saw himself as a frustrated forester who was unfairly denied the opportunity to study forestry in college. He loved his trees, or so he said. Neighborhood gossip had it that he'd once fired a handgun over the head of a woman on horseback who had trespassed in his field and jeopardized some pine seedlings. We stopped speaking altogether after veiled threats of physical violence were made by him against my wife, who one day skied across his back field after a spring snowfall.

A few years ago, the old man hired a logging contractor to cut his acreage. The logger left precious few of his beloved trees standing. In fact, a number of local forest-cutting ordinances were violated. What remains of the old man's once-robust mixed forest is a few birch blowdowns and an expansive berry patch.

Each Christmas, the old man sent us a card urging us to accept Christ. Then this spring, while waiting to have a prescription filled at the pharmacy, I wound up elbow to elbow with the old man.

"How are you doing, Tom?" I asked, breaking a long silence.

He looked frail, and a portable oxygen bottle was feeding plastic tubes in his nostrils. He was not the same man who had kicked me off his property nearly a decade ago.

"Aren't the golden years wonderful," he intoned sardonically. Nothing more was said as we waited together for our prescriptions.

"Take care, Tom," I found myself saying as I left the pharmacy.

About a month later, we saw an ambulance in Tom's yard. In a few days, word got around that our eccentric neighbor had died. His obituary didn't tell the whole story. Soon the house and land were sold, and Tom's wife, who I'd only caught glances of over the years, left with her relatives for good.

Last week, I walked across Tom's woodlot for the first time in a long time without feeling guilty. Although the dark cedar groves and massive pines and hemlocks no longer provide the once-excellent deer cover, the harvested forest has started to regenerate. Softwood seedlings are finding their way through the tangle of alder shoots and raspberry bushes.

Remnants of Tom's big tractor tires remain. Each fall for as long as he was able, Tom would drive his tractor around his logging roads in November, looking for trespassing deer hunters who he could drive off his land.

I picked a quart of sweet, wild raspberries and checked for deer tracks. There were some signs. The berries came hard, but they were worth it. I went back and picked a quart a day for a week. For the True Gatherer, foraging for wild berries on a sunny day when there is an afternoon breeze stirring is a special kind of peace. Especially when you're not on forbidden ground.

Walking home with my hard-earned berries, I wondered. Wherever the old man from Fall River has gone, does he still resent my presence? Were he still alive and struggling for breath, would he begrudge me a few berries and some quiet moments on his land? And what about the new owners of this land, who have yet to move into the old man's house? Will they let me berry, or hunt, or run my dog?

I really hope so.

48

The Sounds of Quiet

In a thought-provoking article about Rocky Mountain meadows in *Bugle* magazine, Scott Stouder makes the observation that "Places where quiet can still be heard are disappearing from our world."

Man, is he on the mark! More than ever it seems that audio stimulation—noise—is the norm for modern society. Wherever we go, whatever we do, our ears are assaulted by the sounds of progress. Cell phones can ring anywhere, in the Amazon jungle or on Pamola Peak on Mount Katahdin. Joggers, with their iPods stuffed in their ears, miss the early-morning songbirds or the rhythm of their Nikes tapping along the asphalt. Soft restaurant conversation is abruptly halted when your dinner companion's cell phone demands attention.

Broadcasters use the term *dead air*. This is when there is no talk or music—silence on the airwaves. It is to be avoided at all costs, which may explain why a caller who is put on hold is never, ever left in silence. Heaven forbid! Musical interludes are always provided. Whether the music is not to your taste or whether you prefer silence to gather your thoughts is irrelevant. The decree has come down from a society hooked on relentless stimulation. You must never be left to your own devices or fed "dead air." *It is written.*

What are the sounds of quiet? How do we measure them? We know how to measure noise, but, as Stouder observed, we have no universal standard to measure quiet. We joke and even write songs about the sound of silence. If a tree falls in the woods and there is nobody there to hear it crash to the earth, does it make a sound? Or the sexist variation on this: If a man speaks in the woods and there is no woman there to hear him, is he *still* wrong?

I have some theories. For me, *quiet* is another name for solitude, and solitude is another name for the outdoors. I don't know about you, but a day spent in a cedar bog waiting for a big buck, or an afternoon of trout fishing on a remote pond, is for me more about seeking solitude than taking home a trophy. Am I the typical outdoorsman? Maybe not. But most of the outdoor folks that I have known find something of value, something rewarding about spending quiet moments in the Almighty's natural cathedral.

The quiet we find out there is not always without sound, however. A few days ago, while ice-fishing with my English setter on a remote Maine lake, I couldn't help but notice. *By golly,* I thought, looking at my dog. *She is tuning in to the silence just as you are.*

The morning sun was inching its way onto the lake, but it was cold, windless, and bright. You could hear a pin drop. And we did, almost. From out of nowhere a chickadee flitted in and

Photo by V. Paul Reynolds

What are the sounds of quiet? How do we measure them? We know how to measure noise, but, as Stouder observed, we have no universal standard to measure quiet.

alighted on the handle of the tote sled. We both heard the air passing under its small wings on its way to us. Above the lake on the beech ridge, we heard a raven and the ice-laden branches giving way to the warming sun. Moments later, under the ice, a fat little splake went for a shiner. When the tip-up triggered twenty yards behind us, we heard the flag spring up to the vertical.

The sounds of quiet. I'm not sure about English setters, but we humans, as contemplative bipods, are meant to find quiet moments for a variety of reasons. You don't have to be an outdoor type to find thinking time, but I can't imagine a life without the outdoor option.

Meantime, I worry about my grandkids' generation. At a time when our sensory circuits are notoriously overloaded, fewer and fewer American youngsters are being introduced to the sights, the sounds, and the silence that await those who spend time in what those of my generation always regarded as the Great Outdoors.

49

Dana for Supreme

In trying to recall his favorite expression, this one comes to mind: "I'll tell you one thing—I sure as hell feel more like I do now than I did a while ago!" He might have said that in the evening during a poker game at deer camp after a shot glass of Ol' Stump Blower. Or he might have said it in the morning after his breakfast cure-all, a long swallow of his own concoction: a mixture of raw egg, horseradish, and Worcestershire.

We were young men then, full of spunk and vinegar, and at deer camp in those days some of us stayed up late and partied hard. He was known to be the last to bed and the first to uncap a bottle, but with an unconventional approach. For him, a happy-hour cocktail was a shot glass of whiskey followed by a short trip to the sink pitcher pump for a chaser of branch water.

Those of us who have spent a week at deer camp with this man during the past thirty-seven Novembers have given him a nickname that he has been unable to shake. We call him "The Supreme." When he was born in Patten, his mother named him Dana. Dana M. Young. But his deer-camp name is more important here, for it is the springboard for the story.

The Supreme is the elected leader of a long-standing Maine deer-hunting organization known as the Skulkers of Seboeis. Like other informal organizations, the Skulkers evolved over the years. At first, the supreme-ship of this hunt club was deemed a joke, a title bestowed on a different member every year just to keep it interesting. Along the way, as we hunted together and enjoyed each other's fellowship, some unexpected social dynamics took place.

The Supreme, who was called "Delightful Dana" in the early days, began to show the qualities of leadership that can bring laughter, cohesion, and contentment to a hunt camp. Dana could cook—I mean, *really* cook. A trained chef who first fed me as the cook at my college fraternity house, his fellow Skulkers began to depend upon—indeed, relish—his culinary skills. The yearly Saturday-night game dinner at camp, which was his baby, became a Skulker mainstay, locked irrevocably into our lore and annual camp rituals.

He could hunt, too. A lifelong outdoorsman who killed his first deer in Patten at the age of nine with a J. C. Higgins .22, he was a skilled hunter, and as woods-wise as they come. His years as a houndsman chasing dogs and bobcats through unholy fir thickets and cedar bogs in the depth of winter were testimony to his stamina and dog-savvy. Before the cat hunts ended, his black-and-tan hounds, Houdini and Bonnie, became legendary in Maine hunting circles. A fifty-five-pound bobcat taken by him and his hounds held the Maine state record for years, and may still hold the title.

His sense of humor didn't hurt his standing in camp either. In fact, his wit and bawdy perspective on life and camp doings spawned a yearly camp award simply called "The Dana M.

Courtesy of V. Paul Reynolds

Dana M. Young, the Supreme Skulker of Seboeis.

Young Trophy." Over the years, each of us has earned the dubious distinction of being the recipient of this trophy. He responded to his first nomination as the Supreme Skulker of Seboeis in an unexpected way. While previous Skulkers had spurned the nomination as a bad joke, he embraced it. Indeed, he ran for the office with vigor and imagination. Although he had no serious competition for the "high office," a political demonstration was secretly arranged by the nominee. At his signal, a platoon of hunters from two neighboring deer camps paraded through our cabin carrying endorsement placards and chanting "Dana for Supreme."

He was elected overwhelmingly to his first one-year term.

That took place sometime around the mid-1970s. Since that time, with one or two upsets in his early years of holding the title, he has maintained an unrivaled leadership hold on the Skulkers of Seboeis. Attempts to unseat him have been half-hearted and ineffective at best.

When he is not serving as Supreme Skulker of Seboeis for one week in November, Dana Young lives in Westminster, Maryland, with his wife Colleen and daughter Erin. Although born in

Patten, he lived for a short time in California and attended Hampden Academy in Hampden, Maine, where he played football and won a Junior Speaking Contest with a made-up ghost story.

He currently manages a Carroll County recreational area. When he's not working in his herb and vegetable garden, or putting up preserves, he can be found fishing the Eastern Shore or hunting deer near his home with crossbow, muzzleloader, or rifle. He is a veteran meat cutter, relied on by his hunt buddies for venison care and processing.

Although his sister Roberta (who lives in Hampden) makes better biscuits, in my opinion, nothing can touch his Supreme's Crock-Pot Quail for taste and simplicity. Here it is:

Supreme's Crock-Pot Quail

1/2 cup each of mushrooms, green peppers, and onions
1 can cream of mushroom soup
1 can cream of celery soup
quail, 3 to 4 birds, halved
1/4 stick butter
cooking sherry, to taste

Brown quail in butter. Sauté the vegetables. Place these ingredients in the Crock-Pot. Add soup and cooking sherry, and cook for eight hours on low in a Crock-Pot.

This November, the Skulkers of Seboeis will gather at deer camp to sing their song and elect a new Supreme for the ensuing year. Put your money on the incumbent.

50

The Baron Is Gone

Even though we know better, we still harbor this expectation that people who reach a near-legendary status will live forever. I remember when Wiggie Robinson celebrated his eighty-fifth birthday. The well-known and always ingratiating Maine Guide told me on his birthday that he was "shooting for one hundred." A vital man of boundless energy, I thought he just might make it.

He didn't.

My friend, the Baron of the West Branch, died unexpectedly while working in his flower garden at his camp on the West Branch of the Penobscot River. Joyce, his wife of sixty years, found him. It was her birthday, and Wiggie had picked some flowers for her that day.

I first met Wiggie when I worked for the Maine Fish and Wildlife Department. I had long heard of the legendary Maine Guide, but we never had shaken hands. When we did, on the

Photo by Diane Reynolds

Wilmot "Wiggie" Robinson
May 18, 1922–June 29, 2007.

porch of his camp, I knew right then that I was in the company
of somebody very special.

We hunted and fished and picked wild mushrooms together. I
finally convinced him to write a monthly column for the *Northwoods Sporting Journal*. At the urging of my boss, Fish and Wildlife
commissioner Bucky Owen, Wiggie and I began to cohost a Sun-
day-night outdoor talk radio program, *Maine Outdoors*. Wiggie,

like me, loved radio, and never stopped being impressed by somebody recognizing his voice wherever he went. Every Sunday night
I introduced him as the Baron of the West Branch. He loved it!

But my fondness for Wiggie Robinson goes far beyond a professional relationship. He was the dearest and best kind of a
friend that you could ever hope for. As a man, he was and will
always be an inspiration for me, a role model for how to live a
life. He was a gentle man, and a gatherer—a gatherer of friends
and a gatherer of wild things to eat: grouse, woodcock, venison,
trout, mushrooms, wild cranberries, you name it. Despite his
gentle manner, Wig was a person with strong opinions and a will
to be heard, especially about fishing slot limits and the abbreviated woodcock season. Always warm and witty, full of energy and
optimism, he was a wonderful companion in a canoe or a turkey
blind. *Boston Globe* writer Tony Chamberlain wrote that Wiggie
looked, moved, and thought like a man twenty years younger.
His life motto, once disclosed to another writer, was "Stay active,
live healthy, and never stop doing what you love."

Wiggie's contribution to the Maine outdoor community is a
legacy. He did much more than guide hunters and anglers.
Everybody he met became his friend. He got involved. He
served for years on the Guides' examining board, was chairman
of the Fish and Wildlife Advisory Council, and was an instigator
of various sportsmen's organizations, including Sportsman's
Alliance of Maine, Millinocket Fin & Feather Club, Maine Trap-
pers Association, and the Maine Bird Dog Club, among others.

His favorite trout fly, the Maple Syrup, is nearly as famous
as he is in Katahdin Country.

The day after Wiggie passed away at camp, I spent some
quiet moments at his woods place, walking around and feeling
Wiggie's presence. Joyce knew that I wanted to do something to
help, so she let me go up and shut off the gas. It's little wonder

that he spent so many hours of his life there. The view of Mount Katahdin and the river is spectacular. And you should see his vegetable gardens!

Most of us don't have a say on how or when we depart this life, but for all the loss we feel, it is comforting to know that Wiggie went out the way he probably would have wanted—with his boots on, working in his gardens on a spectacular June day in the shadow of that big mountain.

The Maine outdoor world has not been quite the same without our dear friend Wiggie, who now paddles the Silver Canoe. We think of him often, and we miss him. We will always be grateful for his friendship and his uncommon capacity to let his love shine through.

51

Giving Thanks for Grandmothers

Nanny was the bearer of tradition and the dispenser of wisdom . . . but her most affecting legacy was her greatest gift: absolute and unconditional love.
—*Jessica and Patricia Burstein*

When I was a kid, Thanksgiving always meant a day at the farm with my grandparents and lots of relatives. To this day, the memories warm my insides like a bowl of hot soup. The mixed smells of mincemeat pie and a turkey roasting in a wood-fired cookstove linger even today.

In the morning, my grandfather and my uncles hunted deer out back of the farm in Rockport. Meanwhile, the womenfolk, guided in the kitchen by my grandmother, prepared the Thanksgiving dinner. By mid-afternoon the men returned from the woods and, after sharing a slug of hard cider in the cellar

Grammy Ryer, (center right), with nine of her eleven children. My grandfather, Fred Ryer, (center left), was a logger and a farmer, when he wasn't busy doing other things. My mother, Helen, the youngest, is seated on her mother's lap. (Photo circa 1919)

with my grandfather, we all sat down at a long table and dug into the best meal of the year.

Most boys who grow up in hunting homes long for the day when they can join the men. And those early Thanksgivings, I, too, yearned for that day. Yet my memory of Grammy Ryer conducting Thanksgiving dinner preparations in her flowered dress and starched apron remains the most vivid. With her snow-white hair done up in a bun, I can still see her hovering over that hot Clarion cookstove in the kitchen of that old farmhouse.

Grammy Ryer, like most grandmothers, was a nurturer through and through. She raised eleven kids. Her kitchen was her place, and it was where she wanted to be. Words of this were never spoken, but as children we sensed her need to show her love by cooking up a storm, and we loved her for it.

Her mincemeat pie made from venison was memorable table fare. The recipe dates back to the 1600s, and, I suspect, came across with one of my Pilgrim relatives trying to escape British tyranny. Unlike some other pies—say, lemon chiffon or chocolate cream—this pie is a real rib-sticker. A hungry Pilgrim could survive all winter on a few of these pies. Here's the old recipe for your (or your grandmother's) consideration:

Grammy Ryer's Mincemeat

5 cups deer meat (neck meat if possible)
7 cups apples
1 orange (skin and all)
1 cup suet
2 1/2 cups molasses
1 1/2 cup white sugar
1 1/2 cup brown sugar
3 cups cider
2 cups vinegar
4 teaspoons salt
4 teaspoons cinnamon
4 teaspoons cloves
1/2 teaspoon pepper
2 pounds raisins

Cook deer meat first and remove from bone. Grind meat, apples, orange, and suet. In large pot simmer deer meat, apples, orange, suet, and remaining ingredients, and cook until glazed over (about three hours). Place hot mincemeat into hot sterilized jars. Makes about 11 pints.

So here's to grandmothers, of yesterday and today. May your Thanksgiving every year be bountiful, and blessed by a grandmother's love and caring, in or out of the kitchen.

52

The True Woodsman

When Millinocket guide Wiggie Robinson died in June
2007 at the age of eighty-five, the Maine sporting community
lost more than a wonderful friend and a sportsman whose life
made a difference. Wiggie represented a way of life that is not
much evident anymore. He was without question a real woodsman, a fast-disappearing breed of rugged individual whose hard-
earned knowledge and woods skills literally changed the face of
this country.

What is a real woodsman?

In a thought-provoking article in *Gray's Sporting Journal*, E.
Donnall Thomas Jr. explores this question. As Thomas observes,
you hardly hear the terms *woodsman* or *woodsmanship* used anymore. Most of us who like to hunt and fish are sportsmen, not
woodsmen. Hunting woodcock in an alder run with your English pointer, fly-fishing a remote trout pond in Aroostook

Photo by Judy Robinson

Katahdin country guide and woodsman Wilmot "Wiggie" Robinson. Was he the last of the true Maine woodsman?

County, or even hiking half of the Appalachian Trail, does not a woodsman make.

A woodsman, Thomas explains, comes by his title only one way: woodsmanship. Either you have it or you don't. A woodsman, says Thomas, knows about "knots, canoeing, fire starting, tracking, wildlife identification, camp cookery, working with dogs and horses, wading streams, staying dry, preparing fish and game for the table, interpreting and analyzing signs, skinning and stretching pelts, sharpening knives, using an ax and crosscut saw, repairing equipment, map reading, backcountry navigation by dead reckoning and compass, never getting lost and knowing what to do when you did."

Of course, America's most renowned woodsmen were Meriwether Lewis and William Clark. Their expedition and the amazing survival feat that it entailed could not have left such an incredible national legacy without a vital component: woodsmanship.

Maybe it is a stretch to compare Wiggie Robinson to a Lewis or a Clark, but they all shared many skills that fall under the common mantle of woodsmanship. Wiggie did a lot more than fish, hunt, and trap. He was a gatherer and consumer of wild things, whether it was fish, venison, wild mushrooms, woodcock, or fiddlehead greens. In Millinocket, his gardening skills were public knowledge. He had so many canoes stashed at remote trout ponds he sometimes lost track of them. He was a cook, a canner, and a wild cranberry jelly maker. He fixed things, and knew how to make do. He knew Katahdin Country like the back of his hand, and all the critters that abound there, big or small. He knew gun dogs, and how to work with them. He told stories.

As Thomas writes, there is also an attitude that defines woodsman. "Real woodsmen are patient and observant. They are comfortable in the woods alone, and when they are in the company of others, their own comfort in the outdoors becomes contagious. They never ignore an opportunity to learn from what they see and hear, but they know that they'll never learn it all."

Wiggie Robinson personified that imponderable quality. He could have crewed for Lewis and Clark. And he would have gotten all the way to the Pacific and back, at least in his younger days. He was a true woodsman.

Does Maine have any other real woodsmen left? I can think of a few, and I'm sure that you can name a couple if you really put on your thinking cap. It would be a worthwhile exercise to identify these real Maine woodsmen and spend some time just talking with them.

Speaking of time, Thomas has a theory as to why the woodsman is disappearing from the American landscape. Time. Lack of time in our frenetic culture may be the culprit. For there is only one way to learn woodsmanship, and that is by spending time in the woods. Lots of time.

You can become a Maine Guide simply by purchasing a Guide's study book or attending classes, but you cannot purchase woodsmanship. And it is this fact that makes the woodsman so valued, so special, and why the inevitable disappearance of every true woodsman from our midst is more than just the loss of the person.

53

Portland Creek "Itch"

Lee Wulff, the late fishing pioneer and American angling icon, lured me to Newfoundland with his book, *Bush Pilot Angler*. In the 1940s and '50s, Wulff pioneered the incredible Atlantic salmon and brook trout fisheries on the then-remote northwestern peninsula of Newfoundland. After reading Wulff's captivating accounts of his bush-flying and salmon-fishing exploits on Newfoundland's fabled salmon rivers, like Portland Creek, River of Ponds, and the mighty Humber River, I yearned to see them. And, perhaps, even to wet a line and feel these historic waters slap against my waders.

In early August my fishing companions, wife Diane and friend Fred Hurley, made the rounds of the little fishing hamlet of Portland Creek, Newfoundland. With the help of some neighbors, we finally found the house that we were looking for. Aster Caines, one of Newfoundland's most renowned veteran guides,

Photo by Diane Reynolds

Newfoundland fishing guide Astor Caines.

and his gracious wife, Ada, answered our knock and welcomed us into their home. We sat around the kitchen table and talked up a storm about fishing, fishermen, and fishing camps. Come to find out, the Newfoundland guide and his wife knew Ray "Bucky" Owen, my former boss at the Maine Department of Fish and Wildlife. Astor had guided Bucky a number of times at a salmon fishing camp in Labrador.

Caines is one of those warm, outgoing, and thoroughly unpretentious outdoorsmen who make you feel that you have known him for years. He agreed to find a guide for the next day for Diane and Fred. (In Newfoundland, most salmon rivers are off limits to nonresidents unless they are accompanied by a guide. The good news, though, is that two anglers may share a guide and the associated expenses.) Since I had caught a number of Atlantic salmon over the years, and Diane and Fred had never known the thrill, I bit my lip and agreed to go guideless and serve as the official photographer. Kevin Caines, a cousin of Aster's, would guide Diane and Fred for a day and a half.

The first afternoon, in an intense drizzle, Kevin worked with Diane and Fred, fishing the Big Pool at Portland Creek. Salmon, big salmon, were porpoising everywhere, but no hookups. That evening, Aster stopped by the pool and said to me, "Gitcher rod, b'y, and we'll give 'er a try, eh?" He didn't have to repeat the invitation. Aster and I fished until dark, and the salmon continued to show themselves, but there was never a hookup. No matter. Just to be there, fishing a fabled salmon river within a hundred yards of Lee Wulff's old cabin fireplace in the company of a legendary Newfoundland guide, whose father had guided the Great One, was the true prize. A fly fisherman's dream.

Caines, for all his charm and easy ways, is serious and methodical on the river. His salmon-angling technique is unlike any I ever saw back in New Brunswick on the Miramichi or the Upsalquitch. The fly, which must be small and sparse such as a Blue Charm or Thunder and Lightning, is tied on with what Caines calls a Portland Creek Hitch. (Lee Wulff was forced to resort to this technique after watching the locals outfish him. They called the knot the "rivveling itch.") This is nothing more than two half-hitches tied around the eye of the hook over the conventional knot (improved clinch, or whatever). And the fly must be fished across the water *a very particular way*. As a Newfoundlander advised Lee Wulff: "That 'itch', sir, makes it rivvel across the top of the water, and that's what our salmon likes." Caines instructed me to cast a line that quarters downstream, and then, with the rod tip up at 45 degrees, to more or less drag the fly throughout its downriver swing, always leaving a small wake.

The next day, guide Kevin took us to a remote salmon pool about thirty miles from the asphalt: the Big Bluie.

Smaller than Portland Creek, this was another of Lee Wulff's favorite salmon waters, a lovely, meandering, stone-bottomed

Fishing the Big Bluie in Western Newfoundland, the author's wife, Diane, plays a nice Atlantic salmon. Guide Kevin Caines is ready with the net.

river with lots of spectacular scenic backdrops and solitude. Before the day was out, Diane and Fred had both hooked and landed their first Atlantic salmon. Fred lost three others, including a fish that would have topped ten pounds. The small Blue Charm and the Portland Creek Hitch worked well.

As much as we enjoyed fishing Newfoundland for salmon and trout, we—die-hard anglers all—were in agreement: The island itself, with its warm people, camping opportunities, unmatched scenery, and rich history, left the deepest impressions of all. We'll go back one day, and you should make the trip if you get the chance.

54

Some Bat Stories

Bats are in trouble. They are dying off at a worrisome rate.

A fungal infection called white-nose syndrome is lethal to bats and spreading among bat populations in eastern North America. According to federal wildlife biologist Mark McCollough, scientists are concerned that our brown bats in Maine could become extinct in fifteen to twenty years. McCollough writes, "Bats are among our most useful wildlife. They consume great quantities of noxious insects such as mosquitoes and blackflies. A bat eats its weight in insects each night, as many as three thousand bugs each night!"

What do *you* think about bats?

I'm not exactly afraid of them, though they are a little creepy, if you ask me. Sort of like snakes. Once, while high on a ladder repairing a camp roof, I suddenly came nose to nose with a napping bat. It squeaked. I gasped. It managed to get airborne

Illustration by Mark McCollough

Confronting the swooping, darting critter in my folks' shower stall, the bat proved elusive. There was no choice. It was the bat or me.

and I managed to stay attached to the ladder. Another time, while at my Branch Lake camp, there came a knock at the door in the wee hours. The unexpected visitor was my dad, who had a camp next door. A self-confessed bataphobic, he was wide-eyed and held a fishing net in a gloved hand. His head was covered with mosquito netting.

"Paul, can you come right over?" he asked.

"Sure, Dad. What's up?" I asked through a haze of sleepiness.

"Bats. Two of them inside the camp," he said with urgency. "I managed to get one to fly back out through the door, but the other one is flapping around behind the shower curtain in the bathroom. Your mother is hysterical!"

His message, by implication, was clear. Having had a bellyful of dreaded bats, he wanted me to carry on in the Branch Lake bat battle. A loyal son, I went to Dad's camp. Mom, visibly upset, had a towel wrapped about her head. I assured her that the bat would not harm her, and that she would soon be safely back in bed.

Confronting the swooping, darting critter in my folks' shower stall, it proved elusive. There was no choice. It was the bat or me. After terminating the intruder with a family-size bottle of Pert, I was seized by a boyish impulse. Call it a flashback to my favorite old movie days. (Stephen King was just a kid. Count Dracula was the rage then.)

Back to the bat battle. Coming out of the camp bathroom with a slight drool and my canine teeth bared like Vincent Price, I told my mother that the bat had nipped me on the neck and that I felt weird. I then snarled. She screamed. My father, who loved a practical joke, convulsed in laughter.

My mother, now ninety-four, has finally forgiven me—I think.

Another time, at our old log camp at Pearl Pond, when my kids were young, a bat was doing 360s just below the rafters in the living area. Nobody could sleep. The kids were petrified. My wife expected me to intervene, which I did. Standing on the kitchen table wielding a large iron skillet, I studied the bat's rhythmic flight pattern: *Whoosh, whoosh, whoosh. Boing!* On the fourteenth *whoosh*, I had deftly slipped the skillet directly into the bat's circular flight path. Radar failure. The bat crashed and burned, and I, the Bat Warrior, became my family's hero.

Massachusetts outdoor writer Randy Julius, who brags about his fearlessness when it comes to handling wild critters of any kind, once had the tables turned on him by a large and unpredictable South Shore bat. He captured with his bare hands a large bat that was terrorizing an elderly neighbor lady in the middle of the night. To impress the neighbor with his Jungle-Jim approach to wild critters, he held up the bat by the wings to show her how harmless it was. Randy then stepped outside to release the bat. The bat apparently took a liking to his captor. As Randy released the bat into the cool night air, it fluttered, did a quick 180, and immediately attached itself to Randy's chest, just below the neck.

"Scared me half to death," recalls Randy.

As McCollough points out, bats have been getting a bad rap over the centuries. Without them, our spring bug season in Maine would be even worse than it is, and look at all of the good stories we would be without. If you have a good bat story, share it with someone.

But not at bedtime.

Now, shut up and *drrrrrrrink your bloooood* . . .

55

Maine's Remote Trout Ponds: A Complete List

Maine's 176 trout ponds designated by the Land Use Regulation Commission (LURC) as Remote Ponds are listed alphabetically on the following pages. Not listed are a number of other Maine trout ponds, not designated remote. Some of these non-remote ponds are habitat for wild native brook trout as well.

Trout anglers discouraged by warming waters and lethargic trout during the dog days of August might want to check out some of these higher-altitude remote ponds. A few of these remote ponds are at altitudes in excess of 2,000 feet above sea level. In fact, one pond in Oxford County is at 3,425 feet. Why is altitude of interest? Because it affects air temperature, which in turn affects water temperature, insect hatches, and fish-activity levels.

Among the 176 remote trout ponds, the highest-elevation ponds are as follows: Aziscohos Pond, 2,100; Cape Horn Pond, 1,900; Clearwater Pond, 1,960; Clish Pond, 1,820; Eddy Pond, 2,625; Helen Pond, 2,050; High Pond, 2,080; Ledge Pond, 2,987; Little Swift Pond, 2,450; Midway Pond, 2,725; Moxie Pond, 2,375; Northwest Pond, 2,090; Saddleback Pond, 2,100; Speck Pond, 3,425, and Tumbledown Pond, 2,660.

The highest-altitude pond, Speck, is a small, nine-acre pond in Grafton Township in Oxford County. Of the 176 designated remote trout ponds, 89 of them are located in Piscataquis County. Please remember that vehicular access of any kind (this includes ATVs) is prohibited into these ponds.

To understand the listing, remember that the pond name is first. The second number is the pond's acreage. Next comes the township and the county. The double-digit number that follows the county corresponds with the page in which the pond can be found in a DeLorme Gazetteer. The last number is the pond's elevation above sea level (altitude).

Alligator Pond 47 TA R11 WELS Piscataquis	42 1510
Aziscohos Pond 12 Magalloway PLT Oxford	18 2100
Baker Pond 10 Bowdoin College Grant W Piscataquis	41 1660
Bean Pond 16 T2 R12 WELS Piscataquis	50 1020
Bear Pond 138 T6 R15 WELS Piscataquis	49 1100
Bear Pond 30 Rainbow TWP Piscataquis	50 1070
Beattie Pond 27 Beattie TWP Franklin	38 1810
Beaver Pond 27 Shawtown TWP Piscataquis	42 1430
Beaver Pond 15 T3 R11 WELS Pisacatquis	50 1240
Benjamin Pond 121 Attean TWP Somerset	39 1260
Big Beaver Pond 45 Rainbow TWP Piscataquis	50 1000
Big Boardman Pond 15 TA R11 WELS Piscataquis	42 1450
Big Minister Pond 15 T2 R10 WELS Piscataquis	50 770

Big Murphy Pond 15 Rainbow TWP Piscataquis	50 1000
Big Muscalsea Pond 14 Russell Pond TWP Somerset	49 1540
Big Notch Pond 12 Little Squaw TWP Piscataquis	41 1617
Big Robar Pond 7 T4 R8 WELS Penobscot	51 850
Big Squaw Pond 91 Little Squaw TWP Piscataquis	41 1500
Birch Ridge Ponds 13 TA R11 WELS Piscataquis	42 1300
Black Pond 147 T15 R9 WELS Aroostook	63 1240
Blakeslee Pond 57 T5 R6 WELS Somerset	39 1740
Bluffer Pond 10 T8 R11 WELS Piscataquis	56 1145
Boulder Pond 30 T5 R7 BKP WKR Somerset	39 1200
Brackett Pond 10 Blanchard PLT Piscataquis	31 1530
Brayley Pond 6 T7 R10 WELS Piscataquis	56 830
Buck Pond 6 Rainbow TWP Piscataquis	50 1253
Campbell Pond 9 T5 R4 NBKP Somerset	47 1900
Cape Horn Pond 30 Prentiss TWP Somerset	47 1900
Cedar Pond 65 TB R10 WELS Piscataquis	42 1100
Cedar Pond 5 Holeb TWP Somerset	39 1320
Celia Pond 9 T3 R10 WELS Piscataquis	50 1240
Chase Stream Pond 31 Misery TWP Somerset	40 1640
Chesuncook Pond 272 T3 R11 WELS Piscataquis	50 1060
Clayton Pond 75 T6 R17 WELS Somerset	54 1470
Clear Pond 21 Lowelltown TWP Franklin	38 1880
Clearwater Pond 11 Prentiss TWP Somerset	47 1960
Clearwater Pond 34 Attean TWP Somerset	39 1275
Clifford Pond 17 Rainbow TWP Piscataquis	50 1210
Clish Pond 16 T5 R20 WELS Somerset	47 1828
Cranberry Pond 7 Bowdoin College Grant W Piscataquis	41 1600
Daisy Pond 11 T2 R10 WELS Piscataquis	50 1050
Dipper Pond 13 Pittston Academy Somerset	48 1670
Dixon Pond 17 Pierce Pond TWP Somerset	30 1320
Doughnut Pond 12 Rainbow TWP Piscataquis	50 1270
Dubois Pond 18 Prentiss TWP Somerset	47 1780

Dwelly Pond 32 T5 R10 WELS Piscataquis   50 1420
East Chairback Pond 50 T7 R9 NWP Piscataquis   42 1510
Eddy Pond 9 Sandy River PLT Franklin   29 2625
Ferguson Pond 63 T14 R8 WELS Aroostook   63 860
Fernald Pond 7 Parlin Pond TWP Somerset   40 1670
First Currier Pond 20 T9 R11 WELS Piscataquis   56 1270
Fogg Pond 21 Bowdoin College Grant W Piscataquis   41 1750
Fourth Roach Pond 266 Shawtown TWP Piscataquis   42 1430
Fowler Pond 19 T3 R11 WELS Piscataquis   50 1270
Gardner Lake 288 T15 R9 WELS Aroostook   63 1150
Gauntlet Pond 11 TB R10 WELS Piscataquis   42 1141
Gordon Pond 28 Upper Enchanted TWP Somerset   39 1560
Gould Pond 12 Rainbow TWP Piscataquis   50 1090
Green Mountain Pond 10 T6 R6 WELS Penobscot   58 1160
Hafey Pond 23 T18 R11 WELS Aroostook   66 1350
Hale Pond 40 Alder Brook TWP Somerset   48 1470
Hall Pond 19 Prentiss TWP Somerset   47 1790
Hall Pond 42 T5 R7 BKP WKR Somerset   39 1150
Harrington Pond 40 T3 R11 WELS Piscataquis   50 1090
Hathorn Pond 15 T4 R8 WELS Penobscot   51 870
Hedgehog Pond 5 T1 R11 WELS Piscataquis   42 1335
Helen Pond 15 Pierce Pond TWP Somerset   30 2050
High Pond 7 Pierce Pond TWP Somerset   30 2080
Holbrook Pond 224 Rainbow TWP Piscataquis   50 1020
Horserace Ponds 50 Rainbow TWP Piscataquis   50 1070
Horseshoe Pond 15 T16 R09 WELS Aroostook   67 1460
Horseshoe Pond 173 T8 R10 WELS Piscataquis   41 1475
Horseshoe Pond 50 Attean TWP Somerset   39 1270
Ireland Pond 30 T7 R8 WELS Penobscot   57 850
Ironbound Pond 43 T3 R3 NBKP Somerset   48 1380
Jackson Pond 23 T3 R11 WELS Piscataquis   50 1240
Juniper Knee Pond 32 Elliotsville TWP Piscataquis   41 1000

Kelly Pond 62 T2 R12 WELS Piscataquis 50 1030
Lane Brook Pond 33 T6 R6 WELS Penobscot 58 1150
Lane Pond 24 Comstock TWP Somerset 48 1690
Lang Pond 30 Parlin Pond TWP Somerset 40 1575
Ledge Pond 6 Sandy River PLT Franklin 19 2987
Line Pond 7 T5 R20 WELS Somerset 47 1870
Little Beaver Pond 10 T3 R11 WELS Piscataquis 50 1230
Little Beaver Pond 8 Rainbow TWP Piscataquis 50 1090
Little Boardman Pond 6 TA R11 WELS Piscataquis 42 1450
Little Bowlin Pond 34 T5 R7 WELS Penobscot 51 760
Little Dingley Pond 17 T4 R5 NBKP Somerset 47 1670
Little Enchanted Pond 27 Upper Enchanted TWP Somerset 39 1862
Little Foley Pond 35 Comstock TWP Somerset 48 1650
Little Frost Pond 35 T3 R12 WELS Piscataquis 50 1020
Little Hathorn Pond 8 T4 R8 WELS Penobscot 51 850
Little Houston Pond 23 Katahdin Iron Wks Piscataquis 42 1099
Little Hurd Pond 60 T2 R10 WELS Piscataquis 50 740
Little Lang Pond 30 Parlin Pond TWP Somerset 40 1575
Little Long Pond 55 T10 SD Hancock 25 230
Little Minister Pond 4 T2 R10 WELS Piscataquis 50 850
Little Muscalsea Pond 11 Russell Pond TWP Somerset 49 1540
Little Notch Pond 10 Little Squaw TWP Piscataquis 41 1617
Little Reed Pond 25 T8 R10 WELS Piscataquis 56 1260
Little Rocky Pond 12 TA R11 WELS Piscataquis 42 1390
Little Squaw Pond 25 Little Squaw TWP Piscataquis 41 1555
Little Swift River Pond 15 Township E Franklin 18 2450
Little Wadleigh Pond 15 T8 R15 WELS Piscataquis 55 1290
Long Bog 19 Holeb TWP Somerset 39 1260
Long Pond 37 Attean TWP Somerset 39 1255
Loon Pond 5 T1 R11 WELS Piscataquis 42 1370
Loon Pond 37 Attean TWP Somerset 39 1300
Lost Pond 5 Attean TWP Somerset 39 1290

Lower 1st St. John Pond 29 T4 R17 WELS Somerset	48 1830
Lower Bean Pond 40 Rainbow TWP Piscataquis	50 1060
Lower Hudson Pond 75 T10 R10 WELS Piscataquis	6 1190
Mary Petuche Pond 10 Prentiss TWP Somerset	47 1780
McKenna Pond 53 T3 R11 WELS Piscataquis	50 1170
McKenney Pond 9 Upper Enchanted TWP Somerset	39 1635
Messer Pond 27 T5 R8 WELS Penobscot	51 670
Middle Bean Pond 10 Rainbow TWP Piscataquis	50 1070
Middle Branch Pond 34 T5 R9 WELS Piscataquis	42 1183
Midway Pond 7 Sandy River PLT Franklin	29 2/25
Mink Pond 19 T14 R10 WELS Aroostook	62 1250
Mountain Catcher Pond 84 T6 R8 WELS Penobscot	57 680
Mountain Pond 56 Beaver Cove Piscataquis	41 1690
Mountain View Pond 13 TA R11 WELS Piscataquis	42 1590
Moxie Pond 6 Township D Franklin	18 2375
Mud Pond 6 Township 6 N of Franklin	19 1150
Murphy Pond 12 TA R11 WELS Piscataquis	42 1230
Murphy Pond 8 Rainbow TWP Piscataquis	50 1000
North Little Black Pond 6 T15 R9 WELS Aroostook	63 1320
Northwest Pond 32 T3 R6 WBKP Franklin	28 2090
Notch Pond 10 Bowdoin College Grant W Piscataquis	41 1860
Papoose Pond 3 Little Squaw TWP Piscataquis	41 1640
Pitman Pond 20 T2 R10 WELS Piscataquis	50 830
Polly Pond 15 T3 R11 WELS Piscataquis	50 1160
Porter Pond 58 T3 ND Hancock	34 450
Rabbit Pond 10 T1 R11 WELS Piscataquis	42 1270
Rabbit Pond 10 Elliotsville TWP Piscataquis	41 1170
Rainbow Pond 17 T3 ND Hancock	34 470
Rainbow Pond 58 Rainbow TWP Piscataquis	50 1040
Redington Pond 37 T1 R2 WBKP Franklin	29 1600
Ripogenus Pond 76 T4 R12 WELS Piscataquis	50 1070
Robbins Brook Pond 18 T12 R11 WELS Aroostook	62 1330

Roberts Pond 19 T5 R20 WELS Somerset	47 1890
Round Pond 5 Appleton TWP Somerset	39 1540
Saddleback Pond 13 Sandy River PLT Franklin	19 2100
Second Currier Pond 28 T9 R11 WELS Piscataquis	56 1290
Second St John Pond 105 T4 R17 WELS Somerset	48 1810
Secret Pond 12 Elliotsville TWP Piscataquis	41 1100
Seventh Roach Pond 33 TA R11 WELS Piscataquis	42 1490
Sixth Debsconeag Pond 31 T1 R11 WELS Piscataquis	50 990
Sixth Roach Pond 48 Shawtown TWP Piscataquis	42 1390
Slaughter Pond 66 T3 R11 WELS Piscataquis	50 1140
Snake Pond 8 Johnson Mountain TWP Somerset	40 1680
Socatean Pond East 42 Plymouth TWP Somerset	48 1370
Socatean Pond West 14 Plymouth TWP Somerset	48 1260
South Little Black Pond 7 T15 R9 WELS Aroostook	63 1280
Speck Pond 9 Grafton TWP Oxford	18 3425
Spring Pond 15 T7 R10 WELS Piscataquis	56 1000
Spruce Mountain Pond 14 TB R11 WELS Piscataquis	42 1770
Squaw Pond 11 Lowelltown TWP Franklin	38 1540
Stratton Pond 15 Rainbow TWP Piscataquis	50 1270
Sunday Pond 30 Magalloway PLT Oxford	18 1425
Third St John Pond 190 T4 R17 WELS Somerset	48 1630
Tilden Pond 36 T10 SD Hancock	25 230
Tobey Pond #1 42 T5 R7 BKP WKR Somerset	39 1210
Tobey Pond #2 30 T5 R7 BKP WKR Somerset	39 1210
Tobey Pond #3 14 T5 R7 BKP WKR Somerset	39 1210
Trout Lake 5 Kossuth TWP Washington	45 790
Trout Pond 55 Lowelltown TWP Franklin	39 1325
Trout Pond 17 Mason TWP Oxford	10 800
Trout Pond 20 Bowdoin College Grant W Piscataquis	41 1240
Tumbledown Dick Pond 25 T1 R11 WELS Piscataquis	42 900
Tumbledown Pond 9 Township 6 N of Franklin	19 2660
Turtle Pond 81 Lake View PLT Piscataquis	43 600

Twin (Trout) Ponds 60 T2 R9 WELS Piscataquis	51	830
Two Mile Pond 12 T16 R13 WELS Aroostook	70	1070
Unnamed Pond 8 T6 R15 WELS Piscataquis	49	1130
Unnamed Pond 5 Attean TWP Somerset	39	1280
Unnamed Pond 12 Attean TWP Somerset	39	1250
Unnamed Pond 10 T5 R7 BKP WKR Somerset	39	1180
Unnamed Pond 2 Holeb TWP Somerset	39	
Unnamed Pond North 15 Comstock TWP Somerset	48	1650
Unnamed Pond South 20 Comstock TWP Somerset	48	1630
Upper 1st St John Pond 30 T4 R17 WELS Somerset	48	1850
Upper Bean Pond 29 Rainbow TWP Piscataquis	50	1100
Upper Bluffer Pond 15 T8 R11 WELS Piscataquis	56	1290
Upper Dingley Pond 20 T4 R5 NBKP Somerset	47	1790
Upper Hudson Pond 25 T11 R10 WELS Aroostook	56	1500
Welman Ponds 45 Prentiss TWP Somerset	47	1680
West Chairback Pond 47 T7 R9 NWP Piscataquis	42	1775
Wing Pond 10 Skinner TWP Franklin	38	1720
Woodman Pond 6 Rainbow TWP Piscataquis	50	1210
Wounded Deer Pond 12 Prentiss TWP Somerset	47	1690